Surf

Fishing

Surf
Fishing

Vlad Evanoff

Illustrations by the author

Harper & Row, Publishers
New York, Evanston,
San Francisco, London

Portions of the text and illustrations in this book appeared in different form in an earlier work by the author entitled *Surf Fishing*, published by Ronald Press Company.

PHOTOGRAPHS: Oregon State Highway Department, title page, ch. 2, 3, 17, 20; Texas Highway Department, ch. 1, 18; Richard Frear/U. S. Department of the Interior, ch. 4; Myrtle Beach, South Carolina, Chamber of Commerce, ch. 5; Vlad Evanoff, ch. 6, 8, 9, 16, 19; Joel Arrington/North Carolina Department of Conservation and Development, ch. 7, 10, 12, 13, 14; Larry Green, ch. 11; FCA Photo, ch. 15.

FIRST EDITION

Designed by Janice Stern

Library of Congress Cataloging in Publication Data

Evanoff, Vlad.
  Surf fishing.
  1. Surf fishing. I. Title.
SH457.2.E95 1974   799.1'2   73-14257
ISBN 0-06-011233-6

This book is dedicated to the many pioneers of modern surf fishing, those who helped develop the rods, reels, lures, methods, and techniques or, through their writings, imparted their know-how to future generations: Hartie Phillips, Leonard Hulit, Gus Kubler, Gus Meisselbach, Julius Vom Hofe, Frank Johnson, Ed Davis, Jack Clayton, Fred Berger, Matt Stratton, Capt. Charles White, Charley Ferrara, Louis Cihlar, Frank Tuma, Van Campen Heilner, Frank Stick, Philip Mayer, Louis Gurriere, Frank Perez, Clayt Hoyle, Charles Beckmann, Lynn Bogue Hunt, Ray Camp, Capt. Bernice Ballance, Otto Henze, Mike Olenick, Jerry Ferrone, Jerry Sylvester, Ollie Rodman, August "Primo" Livenais, Bob Pond, Hal Lyman, Frank Woolner, Stan Gibbs, George Heinold, Claude Rogers, Jerry Jansen, Al Reinfelder, Lou Palma, Milt Rosko.

CONTENTS

FOREWORD

There is general agreement that surf fishing is one of the hardest ways to catch fish. Many anglers have tried it and have given up, turning to easier kinds of salt-water fishing. Surf fishing requires more experience, skill, and know-how than most forms of fishing. It takes a long time to become skilled enough to catch even a fair number of fish from the beach. Many beginners become discouraged when they find out that it usually takes years to acquire the techniques and skills needed to catch fish from the surf.

About the only short cut to learning surf fishing is to have a veteran take you under his wing and let you come along on fishing trips. Unfortunately, however, there aren't too many such old-timers or experts who are willing to do this. What can you do, then?

You can join one of the many surf fishing clubs in the coastal states. Here you will meet other surf anglers who will help you and often invite you on surf fishing excursions. You can also read magazines, outdoor columns, or similar published material to pick up some information. One of the best publications is the *Salt Water Sportsman,* which often runs articles on surf fishing.

However, it will still take a lot of time to acquire all the skills and knowledge needed for successful surf fishing. This book covers surf fishing broadly and at the same time brings out those details that are often overlooked in most material published on the subject. If this work helps shorten the way for the beginner and offers some helpful hints or additional know-how to the veteran surf angler, the author will be satisfied and more than repaid for his efforts.

Vlad Evanoff

ACKNOWLEDGMENTS

The author wishes to thank the following for supplying information or photos used in this book: Canadian Government Travel Bureau; Cape Cod National Seashore; Cape May County Publicity Bureau; Florida News Bureau; Garcia Corporation; Joel Arrington; Larry Green; Myrtle Beach Chamber of Commerce; New York State Department of Commerce; Oregon State Highway Commission; San Francisco Convention and Visitors Bureau; Texas Highway Department; Texas Parks and Wildlife Department; United States Department of Interior National Park Service; and the Woodstream Corporation.

WHY GO
SURF FISHING?

Those anglers who like surf fishing and frequently go out to fish beaches, rocky shores, or jetties do not have to be told about the sport. They already know what surf fishing has to offer and many of them believe that no other salt-water fishing compares with casting into the breakers.

Surf fishing is in no way a new kind of fishing. It goes back to the time when men first collected and ate fish that were washed up on the beaches or speared fish that came into the shallows or got trapped in tidal pools. Later, of course, all kinds of nets, seines, and traps or weirs were used to catch fish in the surf or from shore. These early methods were, of course, used to catch fish for food rather than for pleasure or sport. Records of early hook-and-line fishing in the surf found in many parts of Europe show these early efforts were rather simple and crude. Spanish and French fishermen used a forked sapling; the line was coiled on the sand and then the weight was hurled into the ocean, carrying the line and bait with it. Another device was a kind of tennis racket. The baited hook and sinker were placed on it and flung into the breakers.

In the United States the early settlers in New England were catching striped bass back in 1634. They used a cod line with a piece of lobster for bait; this was thrown into the sea and when a bass took the bait, the line was hauled in quickly and the fish clubbed on the head.

This "heave and haul" method has been practiced down through the years. Various natural baits, eel skins, and metal squids were tossed from the beaches and shores of New England, Long Island, and New Jersey during the 1800's and even early 1900's. A thick hand line with the hook and bait or lure attached was twirled above the angler's head and flung as far as it would go. The line was coiled on the beach, held in one hand, or looped in a basket suspended around the fisherman's neck by a leather thong. With these lines a fisherman could get out 100 feet or so to hook and land striped bass, bluefish, and weakfish.

Surf fishing as we know it really didn't get started until after the Civil War, when wealthy New York and Boston sportsmen traveled to the shores of Massachusetts and Rhode Island to catch striped bass. They founded such famous striped bass fishing clubs as Cuttyhunk, Pasque Island, Squibnocket, West Island, Beavertail, and Graves Point, named for various fishing spots located mostly along the shores of Rhode Island and of Cuttyhunk and Martha's Vineyard off Massachusetts. At one time most of the island of Cuttyhunk was owned by the club of the same name. Some of these clubs were limited to 30 members, each of whom paid a $1,000 initiation fee. Surf anglers were scarce along the beaches and rocks in those days.

These anglers could afford the money to travel to the fishing areas by train or horse and buggy or coach, then lease or buy the land, build fishing stands and clubhouses, and hire people to maintain them. The fishing stands were made of wooden planks over iron stanchions or supports that ran anywhere from 30 to 100 feet out into the water. At the end there was usually a wider platform or a big boulder on which an angler could stand in comfort and safety. A bench or chair was also provided, in case the angler wanted to sit while he waited for a bite. Some of the stands were protected by iron rails. Each evening the club members drew lots to determine which stand they would fish from the next morning since some were considered better than others.

The anglers rose as early as 3 o'clock, and daybreak found them fishing from the stands. A helper known as the "chummer" accompanied each angler to cut up the menhaden or bunker and to bait the angler's hook with a fillet. The rest of the bait fish—head, tail, and entrails—would be chopped up and thrown into the water to create an oily slick to bring striped bass and bluefish within casting distance. (Lobster tails were also used for bait. The rest of the lobster was chopped and thrown out for chum. Small lobsters were plentiful and cheap in those days and you could get a barrelful for a penny apiece.)

Sometimes the bass and blues could be seen swirling on the surface after the pieces of chum. But at other times the men fished blind, casting the bait into the water and then sitting down to wait for a bite. When a fish was hooked the angler would play it up to the platform or rock where his helper would gaff it.

Although plenty of big bluefish were caught, they were considered pests by these anglers, and only big striped bass were desirable. Accurate records were kept by each club, showing the number of striped bass caught each year, their weight, and the names of the men who caught them. Usually a striped bass in the 40- or 50-pound class was the biggest fish for the season, but the records also show fish in the 60-pound class being caught every now and then.

The tackle used by these early striped bass anglers were rods from 7 to 9 feet in length. They were made of greenheart, lancewood, bethabara, Calcutta cane, and bamboo. The reels were oversized models of the fresh-water multiplying or Kentucky reel first made by the watchmaker George Snyder in 1810; they were usually brass or German silver and had jeweled bushings. Lines were braided silk or twisted linen, usually 12 or 18 strands or threads for surf fishing. With such outfits these early striper fishermen were casting baits and lures about 250 feet or even more—not bad when you realize that plenty of present-day surf anglers have trouble getting out that far even with the latest rods and reels.

Around 1900 this exclusive picture changed rapidly as more anglers took up surf fishing. Tackle manufacturers began to turn out rods, reels, and lines at reasonable prices to meet the demand. After World War I, surf fishing became even more popular as cars became available to take anglers to distant spots. Zane Grey was writing about salt-water fishing and Leonard Hulit and other surf anglers were writing about their sport in books and outdoor magazines. In 1924 Van Campen Heilner and Frank Stick wrote *The Call of the Surf,* the first book devoted entirely to surf fishing.

Surf fishing tackle was also greatly improved during this period. Rod makers were making better and longer split-bamboo rods. Reel manufacturers added star drags to surf fishing reels and such models as the Cozone, Perez, Capitol, and Ike Walton were used and treasured by surf anglers. The leading surf reel companies were Edward Vom Hofe, Pflueger, Bronson, and Ocean City. Then along came the Penn Fishing Tackle Company with its popular Surfmaster and Squidder surf reels with light spools, and surf casting became a bit easier.

After World War II, surf fishing really boomed as millions of servicemen returned from the war impatient to wet a line. Fiberglass rods were introduced. The spinning reels that appeared on the surf fishing scene and new braided and solid nylon lines all made surf fishing more productive and efficient.

For a time there was a serious shortage of lures for surf fishing. But lure manufacturers soon developed a great variety of new and killing surf lures—the Flap-Tail, Striper Atom, Popper, Giant Pikie, Darter, and Blue Mullet among others. Anglers started using rigged eels, and catches of big stripers increased in number. Later the plastic eel came along and largely replaced the messy rigged eels.

In the meantime the striped bass population had zoomed and after a long absence the bluefish returned. Almost everyone owned a car and could get down to the beach when the fish were running. Beach buggies, campers, and mobile homes made surf fishing more comfortable and entire families camped and fished along the beaches. The average working man had more money to spend, longer vacations and more holidays, weekends, and time off to go surf fishing.

Those who have never tried surf fishing or anglers who until now have been doing most of their fishing from boats may wonder just what makes surf fishing so appealing. Why do some dedicated surf anglers living hundreds of miles inland travel weekend after weekend and on every holiday and vacation to the beach and, more often than not, return without even a single fish?

Well, surf fishing has many attractions, thrills, and pleasures. It has a lot to offer any angler and it can be tailored to suit any age, sex, or financial position. Once you invest in a surf fishing outfit and the other necessary equipment the cost is very low. There are no boats to own or charter, no gasoline to burn running around in the ocean, no expensive fishing rods and reels to be bought. You can still buy a good surf rod and reel for about $40 or $50. The poor man or man of average means is on equal terms with the rich man. It's not how big and expensive a boat you have, whether you can afford a trained captain and mate, or what kind of fancy tackle you own. In surf fishing, skill and know-how are much more important than equipment. The fish in the surf don't care at all if you're a millionaire or a pauper.

Surf fishing is also very convenient. You can come and go as you please with no reservations for boats or guides. If you want you can fish for an hour or a day or a week. If the fishing is good you can hang around; if it's bad you can pack up and go home. You can fish before work or after work, in the evening or at night when surf fishing is usually best anyway.

There's a challenge in surf fishing. You pit your skill, know-how, wits, and experience against the wily fish and the ocean. There's an element of danger when fishing certain spots—one careless moment and you can be washed off a rock or slip and break a leg.

Most surf fish fight harder than those caught from a boat. They make longer runs and may run you around a jetty or rock or cut your line on barnacles or mussels. And you can't follow them as you do in a boat to gain line or clear your line from an obstruction. You have to stand your ground and try to get the fish through the tumbling surf. The odds are with the fish. When you finally do beach a big one, it's a real accomplishment.

In surf fishing you are on your own—you choose the spot, the lure or bait, the tackle and then cast out, work your lure, hook and beach the fish. It's the individual who counts—you get no help from a guide, captain, or mate. When you have finally landed a fish you did it alone—you can honestly take full credit for the catch and have the satisfaction of knowing that it was due to your own efforts rather than the help of other anglers or a "team" as in big-game fishing.

Surf fishing also offers many thrills and delights; the long casts, nibbles, or smashing strikes of a bluefish or striper, the long runs and tough fights, slippery rocks, and crashing surf are exciting and exhilarating. So is the sight of a flock of screaming gulls wheeling over a school of fish or the fish themselves breaking water while chasing bait. No two days are alike. Every surf fishing trip presents different problems and situations, new thrills and experiences.

Then there is the ever-present suspense and mystery of the sea. You never know what you will hook. It may be a 1-pound sea perch or whiting, or a monster shark weighing several hundred pounds. One surf angler in Massachusetts fishing for striped bass hooked and beached a 180-pound tuna! You'll often fish for hours, then just as you get ready to pack up and quit—wham! a big fish takes your bait or lure. Or a school of fish moves in and the action gets fast and furious.

Surf fishing also offers benefits and pleasures which can be enjoyed even if you don't catch a single fish. Just being on the shore and watching the ocean is restful and satisfying. The surf angler sees and enjoys sights and beauty that other people often miss—colorful sunrises and sunsets, cloud formations; moonlit nights; the greens, blues, and grays of the water, white-capped waves or crashing surf; soaring gulls or diving terns; dunes and white sand. Cool, tangy breezes are very relaxing and make you forget your cares and worries. You return home refreshed and content, ready to tackle the job of everyday living with renewed vigor.

So it's not surprising that today surf fishing is very popular, with every member of the family joining in. Hundreds of clubs have been organized all over the country, from Maine to Florida, along the Gulf of Mexico and the Pacific Coast. The problem nowadays is to find fishing spots open to the public, a parking space, and even fishing room that's not too close to other surf anglers.

SURF FISHING TACKLE

If you are to enjoy surf fishing, it is very important that you get properly equipped with a rod, reel, and line that will perform smoothly and efficiently. Above all, don't try to use makeshift tackle that is not suited for surf fishing. I've seen anglers trying to fish from beaches, jetties, and rocky shores with boat rods, light fresh-water tackle, and other outfits better suited for other kinds of fishing.

You have to take several things into consideration when choosing a surf rod: the area you will fish, the weight of the lures or sinkers you will cast, how far you have to cast, the size of the fish you will catch, and the tides, currents, and waves you will normally encounter.

In other words, where will you be fishing most of the time? Will it be from a sandy beach or a sloping shore? If so, you'll need a somewhat longer and heavier rod than you would use fishing from a jetty or breakwater because long casts are required to reach the best spots. Do you plan to fish a rocky shore where are high cliffs and rocky points and reefs where you can walk out and cast into deep water a short distance away? In such spots you can get away with a shorter rod. Do you plan to fish for small fish using a light lure or sinker? Then you can use a shorter, lighter surf rod. If you go after big fish and have to cast heavy lures you need a longer, heavier, stiffer rod, as you would if you plan to do a lot of bait fishing with heavy sinkers and baits. And when the water is rough and the tides or currents are strong, a heavier rod is best for fighting big fish.

If you fish just one spot or surf fish only rarely, you may be able to get by with only one surf rod. But if you hop from one spot to another or fish often, then you really need two or three rods of different weights and actions.

Today most of the outfits you see are surf spinning rods and reels. They are much easier to use, especially when making casts, and after a little practice a beginner will be casting far enough to catch most of the fish feeding in the surf. Even most veteran anglers prefer these rods and reels because they are less tiring to use, cause no backlashes, and, because of the spinning reel with its fast retrieve, make it possible to work your lures better. A spinning outfit also provides more sport with smaller fish and enables you to cast lighter lures and baits than you can with a conventional outfit.

If you are just starting to fish in the surf I highly recommend that your first outfit be a spinning rod and reel. Later on, after you have been fishing a few years, you can get a conventional rod and reel if you find that you need it in some spots or for some kinds of surf fishing.

Spinning outfits for surf fishing can be divided into three classes: light, medium, and heavy. The light surf spinning rod is from 8 to 9 feet in length and has a fairly easy, limber action for casting light lures and baits. Such a rod can be used with the smaller salt-water spinning reels that hold 200 to 250 yards of 10- or 12-pound-test line. This rod can be used for bluefish, small and medium striped bass and channel bass, weakfish, kingfish (whiting), surf perch, rockfish, halibut, fluke, and most of the other smaller fish caught in the surf. It can cast lures and sinkers from about 1 ounce to 2 ounces or a bit heavier. The light outfit is most practical when fishing from jetties and rocky shores with deep water nearby and when the surf along the beaches is quiet or moderate.

The medium-weight rod ranges from about 8½ to 10 feet in length and comes in various weights and actions, from limber to stiff. Some rods in this class handle lures and sinkers up to 3 ounces. This rod can be used with a medium or even large surf spinning reel holding 250 to 350 yards of 15- or 20-pound-test line and is the nearest thing to an "all-around" surf rod. It can be used from beaches, rocky shores, and jetties in most surf fishing areas. It handles all but the very heaviest lures made for surf fishing. You can also use this rod for bait fishing with the lighter baits and sinkers. If you can afford only one surf fishing outfit or if you fish only occasionally, this is the rod to get.

The heavy surf spinning rod is the choice of anglers who make long casts and use the heaviest lures, baits, and sinkers. The best rod for big striped bass, channel bass, tarpon, small sharks, and other fish up to 100 pounds, it can be used with the largest surf spinning reels holding up to 400 yards of 20- or 25-pound-test line. Such rods range from 10 to 14 feet in length and are the "heavy artillery" of the surf. They can cast lures and sinkers from 3 to 5 ounces, and they make good rods for bottom fishing with bait. You'll see them along Cape Cod and some of the islands off Massachusetts, in parts of Rhode Island, off Montauk, New York, and in Virginia and North Carolina. They are also popular with Pacific Coast surf anglers who have to make long casts from sandy beaches.

The one-handed spinning rod is often used in the Gulf of Mexico or from rock jetties and rocky shores with deep water nearby. It can also be used from sand beaches if the surf is calm or quiet. Ranging in length from 6 to 7 feet, this rod is cast with one hand and used with a light spinning reel with 8- or 10-pound-test line. It comes in actions that enable you to cast lures from about ½ ounce up to 1½ ounces. Naturally such a rod is most practical for small fish and fish up to 15 or 20 pounds.

A somewhat similar outfit is the bait-casting, or "popping," outfit that uses the revolving-spool bait-casting reel and a rod about 6 or 6½ feet in length. The reel is filled with line testing anywhere from 15 to 25 pounds. This outfit is best for short casts, quiet waters, and small or medium fish.

Conventional surf rods also come in light, medium, and heavy actions and in lengths from 8 to 12 feet. Here again, the lighter, shorter, more limber rods are best for short casts, light lures, and smaller fish. The longer, heavier rods are used to cast heavy lures and sinkers long distances and are best for big fish in heavy surf. The conventional surf outfit is also somewhat better for bottom fishing in surf where you have to cast heavy baits and sinkers. Because of the heavier lines used with such outfits you'll have fewer breakoffs when you cast, when you're hung up on the bottom, or when you hook a big fish.

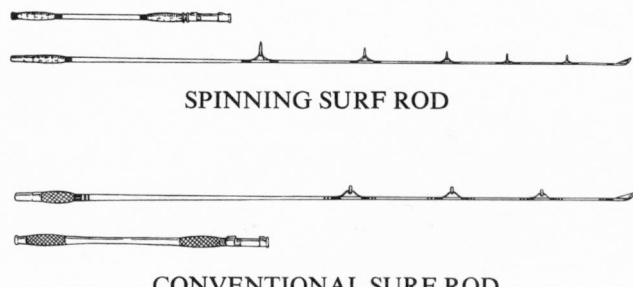

SPINNING SURF ROD

CONVENTIONAL SURF ROD

Should you get a one-piece or two-piece surf rod? Choose the one-piece rod if transportation and storage are not a problem. It is stronger, especially at the ferrules, which are often the cause of trouble in a two-piece rod. But the one-piece rod must be transported outside a car or beach buggy. If you have to travel by train, bus, or subway a one-piece rod is too long. Likewise, if you live in an apartment and have to use an elevator or store your rod in a closet, you'll find the two-piece rod more practical. If you want to keep a rod in your car trunk for instant use in case you get a sudden chance to fish, the two-piece rod is handy.

When choosing a surf rod you also have to consider the butt section or handle. On surf rods most butts range from 20 to 30 inches. The lighter, shorter rods have shorter butts; the longer, heavier rods, longer butts. For most spinning rods, butts from 22 to 26 inches are best. For the heavier, longer, conventional rods some anglers prefer 28- or 30-inch butts. Butts are, however, mostly a matter of personal preference, casting style, and body build. Adults with short arms and children usually cast better with shorter butts. Big men with long arms usually like longer butts.

When choosing a surf spinning reel, match it to the rod you will be using. The smaller sizes are best with light and medium surf rods and the bigger reels are used with the longer, heavier rods. Reels vary in line capacity, depending on the make of the reel, spool size, and strength and thickness of the lines. For most surf fishing even the smallest reel should hold at least 200 to 250 yards of line. The larger models hold up to 350 to 400 yards.

Your surf spinning reel should be one designed for salt-water fishing or even specifically for surf fishing. Then it will have large, strong parts and gears and be made of noncorrosive materials to take the wear and tear of casting, working lures, and fighting fish.

The friction clutch or drag should be smooth and constant. A drag that jerks or binds means broken lines and lost fish. Once adjusted, the drag should hold its position. Today many surf spinning reels have Teflon drags; these are much smoother than drags found on older reels.

Most surf spinning reels have full-bail, automatic line pickups. These are the most convenient and easiest to use if they work properly, but the bails often bend or break or snap shut when you are casting heavy lures or sinkers. Thus many expert anglers prefer manual pickups. You can buy a big spinning reel with a bail pickup and later replace it with an inexpensive manual pickup. Remember, however, that it takes a bit more time to learn how to use a surf spinning reel with a manual pickup and that you do have to pick the line up with your finger so that it is caught by the rotating pickup roller.

The roller over which the line runs when it is being retrieved should be made of a hard substance, preferably very hard metal, sapphire, or agate. The continual retrieving of lures or sinkers and playing of fish will cut grooves in the roller if it is made of a soft material. If the roller is supposed to revolve, it should do so freely.

A good surf spinning reel should also have an anti-reverse lock to prevent the handle from turning backward. Many anglers fish with the anti-reverse in the "on" position most of the time when casting lures or even bait fishing. A good surf spinning reel should also have a big handle knob that is easy to grab and hold.

Several good surf spinning reels, both domestic and imported, are on the market. If you buy a reel made by a reputable manufacturer or importer and if an expert surf angler recommends or uses it, you can be quite certain that it will perform well and stand up in surf fishing. And you can be quite sure that parts are readily available and that the reel can be repaired quickly.

It's always a good idea to have spare reels on hand when you go fishing. Surf fishing is tough on tackle of any kind, so always carry a spare rod or two, a spare reel, and plenty of line and lures in the car or have them nearby whether in a motel or at home. It's also a good idea to have lines of different strengths for different fishing conditions and an extra loaded spool or two for your spinning reel so you can have more line ready if you need it.

When it comes to choosing a conventional surf reel you have your choice of several good models that have stood the test of time. Those imported by the Garcia Corporation, such as the Ambassadeur 9000, 7000, and 10,000, are favored by many surf anglers. The Squidder and Surfmaster reels made by the Penn Fishing Tackle Company are old-time favorites. Under most conditions a surf reel that holds 200 yards of line is sufficient; for heavy fishing and for long casts or bottom fishing you may need a somewhat larger reel capable of holding 250 to 300 yards of line.

Lines are a vital part of the surf angler's equipment and give more trouble than any other single item of fishing tackle. Long and constant casting, sand, rocks, mussels, barnacles, surf, big fish, all subject the line to a terrific amount of wear, tear, and strain. Surf anglers are always breaking or cutting lines, fraying or nicking them, or weakening them and losing lures, sinkers, and fish.

The silk, cotton, and linen lines used by early surf anglers were never too good and just couldn't take the wear and tear of surf fishing. After World War II, Dupont came out with braided nylon lines. Used mostly with conventional surf reels, these lines replaced the linen lines then in use, and braided nylon and braided Dacron lines are still favored by many surf anglers who use conventional reels. Dacron lines have less stretch but tend to be drier and even when wet burn your thumb on a long or hard cast. However, they are thinner than braided nylon, so you can get more line on your reel. For conventional surf fishing, lines testing 27, 36, and 45 pounds are the most popular.

When spinning tackle became popular, surf fishers tried the braided nylon lines, but soon replaced them with the single-strand monofilament nylon lines. The first mono lines were thick, stiff, and springy and had a high-gloss finish and a lot of stretch. But they have been improved and are now thinner, limper, and less stretchy; they are made in dull finish or colors which are less visible.

Many domestic and imported mono lines are on the market. Garcia's Bonnyl and Platyl lines are popular and so are the Stren lines put out by Dupont. Some lines can be bought at bargain prices; but you get what you pay for and if you want a limp, good quality, smooth-casting, thin line you have to pay more for it.

Some surf anglers fishing with conventional reels also like to use monofilament 25- or 30-pound-test lines on revolving-spool reels. Here again, line that is soft and limp will usually cast well on such a reel. But you'll have to spool the line on the reel evenly and have an "educated thumb" to prevent backlashes when using these lines.

For spinning you can use mono lines testing from 10 to 18 pounds for light- and medium-weight spinning rods and lines testing up to 20 or 25 pounds for the heavier spinning outfits. Today, because of thinner diameters, you can use a line a few pounds stronger and still get enough line on your reel. In spinning, the thinner the line, the more distance you'll get when you cast.

Although mono lines are tougher than braided lines and do not rot or require drying and constant care, you still have to examine them carefully and frequently for fraying, nicks, and weak spots if you do a lot of casting and fishing, especially along rocky shores or from jetties.

No matter what kind of line you use in surf fishing it is almost a must to tie a "shocker" leader ahead of your regular line. If you use a braided nylon or Dacron line on a conventional reel you can use a monofilament line as the shocker or leader. This can test about the same or a few pounds more than the fishing line being used if you are going to cast mostly lures. For bait fishing on the bottom with heavy sinkers many surf anglers like to use shocker leaders testing up to 50 or 60 pounds.

With a surf spinning outfit you can use a shocker leader testing from a few pounds to 40 or 50 pounds, depending on where you will be fishing and whether you will be casting light lures, heavy lures, or sinkers and baits. The shocker leader should be long enough so that it runs from the lure or sinker through the guides and so that several turns can be reeled on the spool when you are ready to cast.

A shocker leader will save a lot of lures or sinkers that otherwise would be lost during a cast. It also takes the wear and tear when the line rubs on rocks, mussels, barnacles, or the sand in the surf and takes a lot of the strain off the line when you get the fish close to a jetty, a rocky shore, or the breaking surf. Often you can lift a small fish with the leader when fishing from a high rock or jetty. With braided line the monofilament shocker leader is less visible than the fishing line.

One of the best knots for tying the main fishing line to the shocker leader is the "double surgeon's knot." It is quick and easy to tie. Simply lay the end of the line and the end of the leader next to each other and let them overlap a few inches. Holding both lines together, tie a simple overhand knot, then tie another through the same hole. Each time pull the shocker leader through the hole or loop. Finally grab both ends and pull to tighten the knot. You can clip the ends short. This knot won't slip even if you use lines and leaders of different diameters and materials.

When you finally assemble your tackle, you can start to practice casting. Casting with a spinning reel is so simple that in a short time almost anyone can learn to cast far enough to catch fish. Just ask any surf angler to show you the first steps or watch some experienced casters at work on the beach and try to imitate them. Read the instruction booklet that comes with your fishing reel and learn how to operate the reel. Many of these manuals or fishing catalogs show the various casting positions and steps in casting.

Casting with a conventional surf reel is harder and just reading about it won't be of much help. You'll have to go out and practice day after day until you master the "feel" and "timing" of surf casting. This may take a few weeks or months or even years, depending on how often you fish or practice.

As suggested earlier, if you are getting your first surf fishing outfit buy a spinning rod and reel. You'll learn to cast much sooner and can then spend your time learning which baits and lures to select, how to use them, and how to locate the best fishing spots and find fish. These techniques—not casting—are the hardest part of surf fishing, and this book is devoted to passing on such surf fishing know-how.

3

OTHER TACKLE, GEAR, AND ACCESSORIES

When you have bought a rod, reel, line, and even lures you are still not ready to go surf fishing. You need other tackle and odds and ends of accessories to be fully equipped and ready for anything that might happen. Many novice surf anglers skimp on some of these items, figuring they are not really necessary. Then they wonder why they don't catch fish like the veteran surf anglers. For example, I've seen many surf anglers wear boots in areas which call for waders. Then they find that they can't wade out far enough to reach the fish, or they get water into their boots and have to quit fishing or fish in discomfort.

But before we go into clothing and other gear let's cover a few more items of fishing tackle that every surf angler should have at home or, better yet, in his car or beach buggy right on the beach. You should have some wire and nylon leader material in various strengths for making up leaders or rigs, especially if you plan to do some bottom fishing with bait.

Wire leader material is handy if you fish in areas where bluefish, sharks, king mackerel or Spanish mackerel, and barracuda are plentiful. These fish have sharp teeth and can easily cut through lines or leaders made of monofilament or other soft material. Single-strand stainless steel is the most popular wire leader material, and it is available in coils of various strengths and tests. For surf fishing No. 8, 9, and 10 wire leaders are the most practical. To make your own leaders with this wire you'll need side-cutting, flat-nosed, and round-nosed pliers.

The other kind of wire leader is the cable type which comes either bare or covered with nylon or other plastic. To make loops for attaching snaps, swivels, or hooks to cable wire, the wire must be crimped with special crimping or swaging pliers. A small brass or copper sleeve or tube is used for this. Cable wire also comes in various thicknesses and strengths. For surf fishing use the lightest wire that is strong enough to hold the fish you are going after.

However, most surf anglers are getting away from wire and are using monofilament material for leaders or making rigs because such leaders are less visible to the fish. This comes in various strengths but if you get coils or spools of mono nylon in 20-, 30-, 40-, 50-, and 60-pound tests you'll be able to meet most fishing conditions.

The surf angler who plans to do a lot of bottom fishing or use live baits needs a good assortment of hooks. The Eagle Claw type hook is good for bottom or bait fishing and you should have it in sizes No. 2 to 4 for small fish, up to 7/0 or 8/0 for the larger species. A more expensive hook preferred by some striped bass and channel bass fishermen is the Octopus pattern made in England by Edgar Sealey & Sons, Ltd.

The old-time favorite of the surfman is the O'Shaughnessy pattern which is still good and is used in various sizes. The Sproat hook can be used for many of the smaller species. And there are specialized patterns such as the Virginia for blackfish or tautog, the Chestertown for flounders, and the Carlisle or Pacific Bass hooks with their long shanks for fluke or summer flounder.

The best hooks for surf fishing have a finish which doesn't rust too quickly—tinned hooks, cadmium-plated hooks, gold-plated hooks, or hooks made from Z-nickel or stainless steel. If you intend to use a hook only once or twice and then dispose of it, buy bronzed, blued, or nickel-plated hooks. But never use hooks that are badly rusted or have been lying around for a long time and look weak. They can snap or break and lose you a big fish.

Surf anglers use a great variety of sinkers but for sandy beaches the old-time pyramid sinker is still one of the best. Another sinker for beach fishing is the bulldozer, which is shaped like a Y and used along the Pacific Coast for holding in the sand. Along rocky shores or in other areas where sinkers get hung up readily, a better choice would be the round, egg, and bank types. Anglers fishing along rocky West Coast shores often use small cloth bags filled with sand or pebbles as sinkers because if they get lost they haven't cost much.

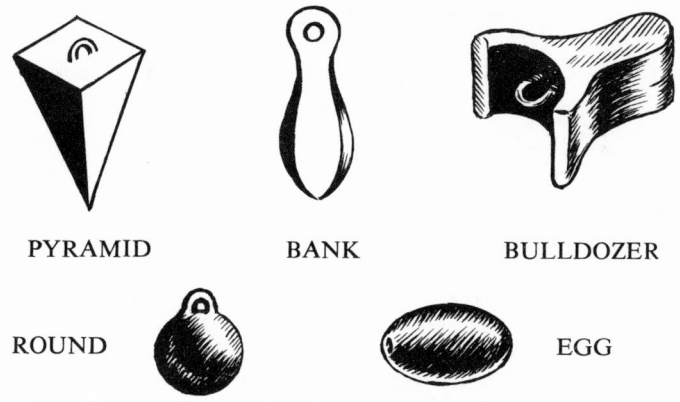

PYRAMID BANK BULLDOZER

ROUND EGG

SINKERS USED IN SURF FISHING

Then there are the various kinds of snap swivels, barrel swivels, three-way swivels, and fish finders. For quick-changing lures I like to use a snap swivel on the end of my leader—for example, the Pompanette or a similar type made by a good company. An assortment of barrel swivels and three-way swivels comes in handy for tying bottom rigs. And the fish finder with a ring on one end and a snap on the other is preferred by many surf anglers for bottom fishing. In rocky areas you can use the egg sinker, which has a hole in the center. The line runs freely through the sinker and fish don't feel the drag of the weight.

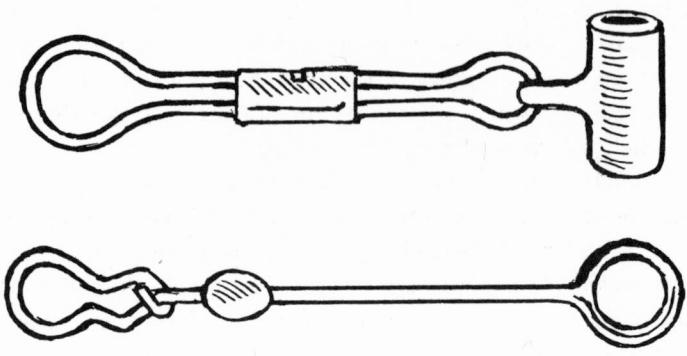

TWO TYPES OF FISH FINDERS

When it comes to waders the surf anglers who fish a lot prefer the fairly heavy all-rubber type, such as the Ball Band and Hodgman made especially for surf anglers. Avoid the commercial black rubber waders used for sewer or construction work or by commercial fishermen. These are too heavy for sports fishermen.

All rubber waders are expensive, but they provide protection and warmth and allow you to wade out on sand, rock, or mussel bars up to your hips. When you buy waders make sure they are on the loose side and that they fit even over heavy pants and socks. Try them on for size to see if you can raise your legs with ease and do knee bends freely. If not, get a slightly larger pair since you'll have trouble walking and climbing rocks with tight-fitting waders.

Plastic waders can also be used for surf fishing, especially if you do most of your fishing along sandy beaches or in warm climates. Although light and less expensive, they don't stand up well enough around rocks, barnacles, or mussels to be used along rocky shores or on jetties. Plastic waders are usually worn with tennis shoes, sneakers, or wading shoes. Since they are not too heavy, not lined, and not insulated, plastic waders are not good in chill northern waters or in cold weather.

On southern beaches anglers often do not wear waders at all during the day. They fish in bathing suits or chinos and sneakers. I wouldn't recommend bare feet when surf fishing because there's always the chance of stepping on broken glass, clam shells, coral, or sting rays or getting stuck by the fins of a fish. And you may step on a hook, lure, or other sharp object.

There is still a place for hip boots in many areas. Hip boots can be used on sandy beaches when the surf isn't too rough. And many anglers fishing from rock jetties like to wear boots. But even here it's a good idea to wear a pair of waterproof overalls over the boots to keep the waves and spray from getting inside.

When fishing along sandy beaches on warm days you can often wear just a shirt or an ordinary jacket. But when fishing at night or in cold weather or the rain or when wading out on a bar, you should wear a waterproof parka over your waders. It should have a hook and drawstring or snaps around the neck, wrists, and waist to keep the water out.

For fishing jetties, breakwaters, rocky shores, or other slippery spots you need a pair of ice-creepers or wading sandals. Even with this protection it's tough to keep your footing on a small rock while casting; it can be dangerous. Ice-creepers and wading sandals can be bought in many coastal fishing tackle stores. The best kind are those with hobnails or short spikes to dig into the rocks or wood.

One of the handiest items a surf angler can have is a web pistol belt; these are sold in many Army-Navy surplus stores or sporting goods stores. These belts have reinforced holes scattered along their length for attaching various items. Many surf anglers fasten to the belt a permanent brass hanger plate with snaps and holders for a fish stringer and a gaff. If you use a flexible telephone cord to hold the short gaff you can extend it to any length when gaffing a fish.

Small pouches or canvas bags can also be bought in Army-Navy surplus stores and these can be attached to the web belt. Pouches can hold the smaller lures such as metal squids, jigs, and plastic eels. For the larger plugs, some kind of light plastic or metal box with separate compartments for each lure can save time and fumbling. The whole idea is to have everything you may need on the belt or in your pockets so that your hands are free when walking, casting, fighting a fish, or climbing rocks and jetties.

The beach fisherman who does a lot of bait fishing or spends the entire day in one small area will find a large shoulder bag handy. This should have a wide strap and enough room to carry sinkers, hooks, rigs, spare reel, and other items. Plastic pails, bait buckets, and styrofoam containers are good for keeping bait fresh or keeping water, soda, or beer cold. And, of course, a folding chair or stool is good for sitting while waiting for a bite.

The bait fisherman also needs a sand spike, a tubular receptacle affixed to a pointed shaft, which is stuck into the sand. The spike is used for holding the rod upright while the fisherman is waiting for a bite or changing baits and rigs. It serves to keep the reel off the sand. The regular short sand spikes will serve along most beaches where they are used on dry land. But when you have to wade out some distance from shore to fish you need the extra long sand spikes known as "staffs" which can be used in shallow water.

Bait fishermen will also find a rod belt helpful for holding a rod high while waiting for a bite. Even anglers using lures find such a belt a big help. The weight of the rod is taken off your hands and arms and it's less tiring to fish this way. The rod belt also helps to take the strain off your arms and groin when fighting a big fish. A rod belt with a wide leather backing or "apron" is best suited for surf fishing.

If you're planning to wade out some distance from shore and don't want to come back to dry land every time you catch a fish, you'll need a fish stringer. You can carry a chain-type stringer on your belt. Stringers can also be used when fishing from jetties

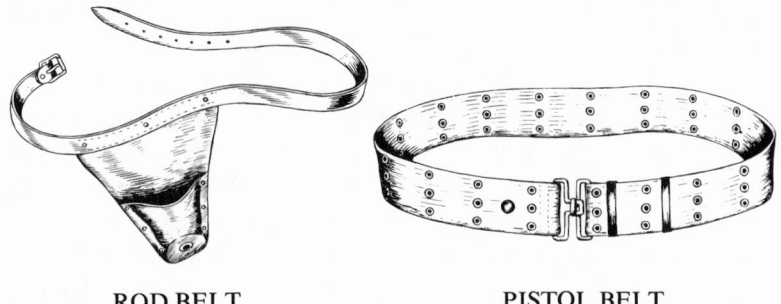

ROD BELT   PISTOL BELT

or breakwaters and along rocky shores to tie a fish down securely so it won't be washed away or to carry several small fish off the rocks or shore. Even along a sandy beach you'll find it easier to drag a good catch or a heavy fish in shallow water or on the sand with a stringer. Here you can use ordinary clothesline, nylon cord, or anchor rope. For this purpose the stringer can be anywhere from 8 to 10 feet long.

A flashlight or lamp can be carried down to a sand beach when bait fishing at night. But when fishing with lures, especially from jetties or rocky shores, a headlight is much better. The type to get is one which has an elastic band to be worn around your neck and a wire running to a battery case on your belt. It leaves your hands free for casting, changing lures, knot tying, fighting fish, and gaffing fish and for walking or climbing safely on jetties or rocks.

A gaff hook is a big aid when you're trying to beach a big fish or when you're fishing from an elevation. For fishing from sand or rock or mussel bars where you wade out into the water, a short gaff attached to your belt with a flexible cord is best. It should have a guard covering the point so that you don't get stuck by accident.

When you're fishing from a rock jetty, breakwater, or cliff you need a long-handled gaff. These can be anywhere from 6 to 10 feet in length. The longer the handle the safer you'll be reaching for a fish when the big waves are breaking. These gaffs should also have some kind of safety guard to cover the point and to keep the point sharp and ready for instant use.

You'll also need a knife for cutting bait, line, hooks out of a fish, and for cleaning fish. A knife that can be carried in a sheath or on your belt is good, but at the least you should have a folding pocket knife. A stainless-steel knife with a fairly long blade made especially for fishermen is best. These knives usually come with a scaler, hook remover, and even a small sharpening stone on the handle for hooks. Whatever knife you get, make sure it will hold an edge and then keep it sharp at all times.

Other handy items are cutting and gripping pliers, a small can or tube of oil, a sharpening stone, insect repellent, sunglasses, and a pair of binoculars. The binoculars usually aren't carried down to the beach but are kept in the car to spot breaking fish or diving gulls and birds.

If you haven't done much surf fishing, you may wonder whether you really need all this equipment. Well, the sooner you get all the equipment you need the sooner you'll be able to catch fish in the surf. Why handicap yourself by being only partially equipped? Surf fishing is tough enough without making it even tougher. And most surf fishing is done quite a distance from home or a tackle shop. When the fish are hitting you haven't got time to get what you need. By the time you drive back and find it or buy it the fish may be gone. The smart surf angler brings along everything he thinks he will need to catch fish in the surf.

LURES

One of the biggest problems facing a surf angler is choosing the right lures. He has to make up his mind just which ones to buy and which ones to take with him. Of course, it is easier for the veteran surf angler or the surf angler who fishes in only one spot most of the time. He usually knows which lures produced best under which conditions and at which times. But even such an angler must narrow his choice and make some compromises because you can carry just so many lures in your tackle bag or belt pouches. And no matter where you fish you should have a good assortment of basic surf lures available because you never know which lures the fish will want on a certain day, what kind of fish will show up, or just what kind of weather and water conditions you will run into.

The metal squid, one of the first lures used in surf fishing, is still popular and productive. Metal squids come in many shapes, sizes, and weights, from ½-ounce models for small fish and light tackle to 4- or 5-ounce squids for heavy tackle and long casts.

The typical metal squid has a keel like a boat and a flat top and is designed to look and swim like some of the baitfish or small fish found in the surf. The small, narrow types imitate sand eels and spearing or silversides. The larger, broader squids imitate herrings, shiners, anchovies, sardines, mullet, and small menhaden.

There are two basic types of metal squids—one with a stationary hook molded into the body of the lure and the other with a swinging hook attached to the squid by a pin, eye, or split ring. Both types are equally good.

Years ago most metal squids were molded from block tin because it was cheap and abundant. Some lead was usually added to make the tin less brittle and less likely to break when bent. Block-tin squids can be polished with steel wool or even damp sand until they shine like silver. And because tin is lighter than other metals, squids made of it have better action in the water when reeled at slow speeds. Tin squids can also be bent easily to improve their action. But today the high price of block tin and the difficulty of obtaining it have made tin squids scarce.

METAL SQUIDS

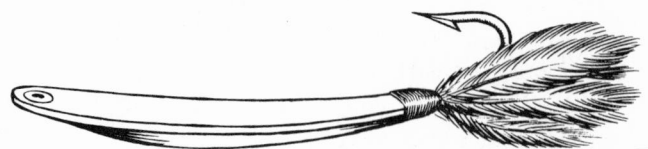

SAND EEL SQUID WITH FEATHERS

MULLET SQUID WITH SECOND HOOK

METAL SQUIDS

SAND EEL SQUID WITH PORK RIND AND TAIL HOOK

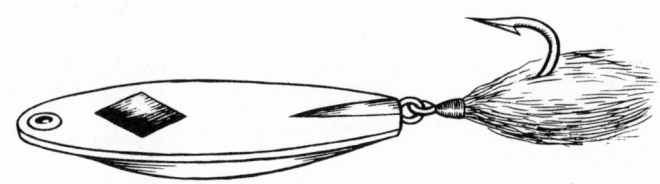

MULLET SQUID WITH SWING HOOK AND BUCKTAIL

Now most metal squids are made from other metals and are either nickel-plated or chrome-plated. If designed properly, with the right action, they are good and take many fish. But because the metals used are hard they usually can't be bent like block-tin squids to improve the action.

Metal squids can be painted in various colors. This is usually done to squids cast from lead, because this metal turns black with time and a white or yellow squid is more visible in the water. You can also paint a lead squid with silver or aluminum paint to brighten it. The hook on a metal squid can be wrapped with white or yellow feathers or bucktail, which will also make it more visible and attractive. Or you can put a white or yellow strip of pork rind on a fixed-hook squid.

Other metal lures used in surf fishing include the heavy spoon-type lures. One of the most effective of these is the well-known Hopkins No-Eql, made of stainless steel with a hammered scale finish. It is available in various sizes and weights and has attracted many kinds of fish in the surf. The No-Eql comes with a treble hook, double hook, or single hook and casts like a bullet. This is one metal lure that can be made to travel on top of the water when reeled fast. For this reason it is a great lure to use in shallow, rocky areas where lures that travel deeper get hung up.

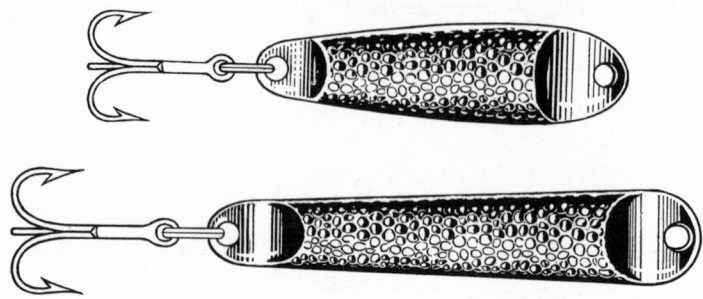

HOPKINS NO-EQL LURES

Another favorite with surf anglers is the Kastmaster, made by the Acme Tackle Company. It has a tapered oval shape that gives it an erratic action attractive to many surf fish.

Surf anglers fishing along the Pacific Coast for striped bass use the Spoofer lure, another flat, metal, spoon-type lure with good action. Still another lure used by West Coast surf anglers is the Sleekee, a short slab of shiny metal with sharp angles on both ends; it casts well and has good action.

Metal lures are especially effective for the small and medium striped bass, bluefish, channel bass, mackerel, and bonito. The lighter types are also good for weakfish and sea trout. Metal lures work best when the surf is fairly rough with plenty of white water and they are essentially a daytime lure. They are also invaluable on days when you have to get out to reach the fish or cast against a strong wind.

It is and always has been difficult to fool big striped bass with metal squids; even the smaller fish often won't hit the metal lures too readily if the water is calm and clear and there is little surf. And, of course, at night, metal lures aren't too effective. Then some surf anglers tried fresh-water plugs, especially the larger, stronger models used for pike, muskellunge, and big black bass. They proved to be killers for striped bass, bluefish, weakfish, and many other surf fish and today no surf angler would go down to the beach without a varied assortment of plugs.

Surface plugs create a splash, commotion, or ripple on top of the water and are very effective. Most baitfish swimming in the surf or being chased by larger fish tend to come to the top and skitter or scatter or splash on the surface of the water. Thus most gamefish are attracted by surface commotion.

One of the best surface plugs is the popper type, which usually has a cupped or slanted head cut at an angle. When the plug is reeled fast and jerked, it throws a splash that drives most fish crazy. Popper plugs are now made by many lure companies in various sizes, weights, shapes, and colors or finishes. Those weighing 1 to 2 ounces are best for small fish and light tackle. The larger models weighing 3 to 4 ounces can be used for bigger fish and with heavier tackle. Most popping plugs have thick, straight or tapered bodies, but one—the Pencil Popper made by Stan Gibbs—is slim and tapers gradually. When reeled and worked fast, it has a weird side-to-side action that most fish can't resist.

Another surface plug that has accounted for many surf fish and is especially good for big striped bass is the swimming type. Most famous of these is the Striper Atom in the big size. The Jr. Atom is a smaller version of this plug. Unfortunately the large Atom is no longer being manufactured.

Swimming plugs usually have a flat metal lip that makes them swim on top in a slow, snaky action leaving a wake or ripple that attracts fish. They can be jerked every so often to throw a splash. These lures are killers day or night.

Another surface plug is the cigar- or torpedo-shaped plug. The Zara Spook plug made by Heddon is a good example. This plug has to be worked fairly fast with plenty of rod action to make a commotion on top and travel in a swaying side-to-side action.

The next class of plugs used by surf anglers are the underwater

PLUGS

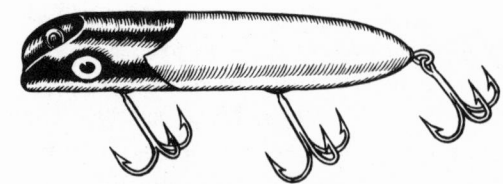

WOBBLER

DARTER

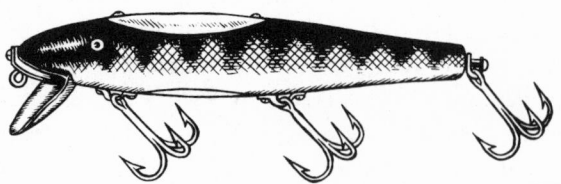

SMALL UNDERWATER

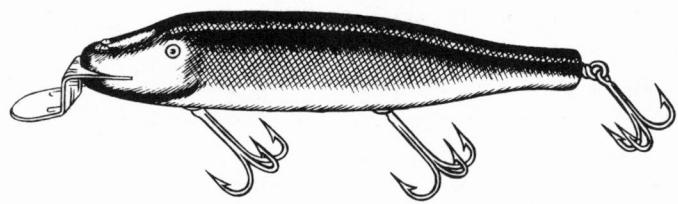

LARGE UNDERWATER

PLUGS

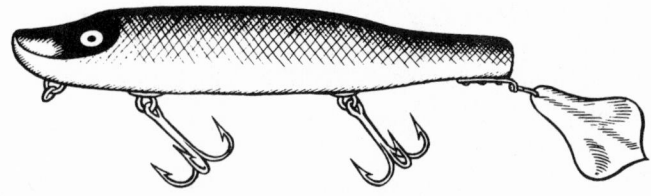

FLAPTAIL

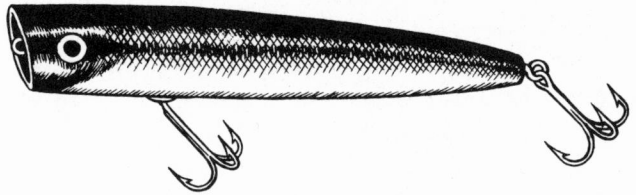

POPPER

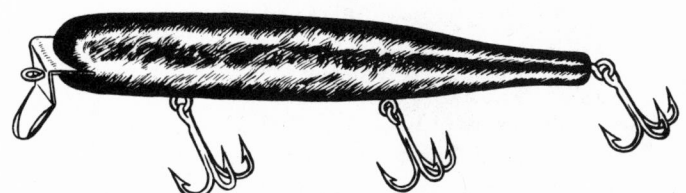

SURFACE SWIMMER

JOINTED EEL

types and, as the name implies, they travel from a few inches below the surface to several feet down. Some of these plugs have grooved or slanted heads that make them dive and dart or wobble from side to side. Some have plastic or metal lips that also cause them to dive and wriggle in an enticing manner. They may have a single body or be jointed. The Creek Chub line of Pikie underwater plugs in various sizes and weights has been used by surf anglers for many years.

Recently balsa wood or light plastic underwater plugs such as the Rapala and Rebel have proved very effective. Usually colored silver or gold, they have a very lively, lifelike action resembling a live baitfish swimming through the water. And they have this action even when reeled at slow speeds. Their main drawbacks are their light weight and low wind resistance, which make them difficult to cast any distance. But they can be used effectively from jetties and breakwaters, rocky shores, rocky points, and sharply sloping beaches with deep water nearby. Or you can use them when fish move right into the breakers to feed.

Other underwater plugs with a natural fishlike finish are the flat types such as the Mirro-lure and Salty Boogie, that look like real baitfish. However, these plugs do not have a built-in action so they have to be worked with the rod to make them act alive.

When choosing plugs for surf fishing try to imitate the size and color of the baitfish found along the beach or shore at the time. Thus, if mullet are moving along the beach use silver or blue finish plugs. In fact, most of the baitfish found in the surf usually have white or pale yellow bellies, silver sides, and blue, green, brown, or black backs. Thus plugs in these finishes will imitate more than one baitfish.

Years ago surf anglers generally used a live eel rigged with one or two hooks for big stripers. These rigged eels are still killers for big striped bass, but they are a lot of trouble to find, rig, preserve, and carry. The eels can be rigged with one, two, or even three hooks, which usually protrude from the belly or underside.

You can do this with a long needle and strong line or flexible wire; the best way to learn how is to have someone show you. Personally I prefer to rig my eels with two hooks, one at the head and the other a few inches from the end of the tail. Some anglers like to add a small metal squid or metal plate at the head so the lure has more weight for casting and better action. In rocky areas, however, I prefer the plain eel. I think it rides higher over the rocks without sinking too fast in shallow water and doesn't hang up as often. And you can work or reel it much slower than an eel with a weight or metal squid up front. But if you're fishing along sandy beaches or in strong tides and rips, the weighted eel will travel deeper and can be used. I also like to use an eel with an action head in the daytime, when I think it is more effective than the plain eel.

Earlier surf anglers fishing in New England liked to use an eel bob or eel tail for striped bass. For these lures the head of the eel is removed and a lead weight is inserted under the skin to provide casting weight. The skin is then tied in front of the lead so it stays in place. These lures are still good and are used occasionally, but they have to be reeled and worked faster than the whole eel, especially in rocky areas or shallow water.

Various kinds of eel-skin lures are also used in surf fishing. The lead-head skin jig is the basic lure of this type. These are molded with one or two hooks on a wire or cable leader. The lead head up front has a groove or ring around it to which the skin is tied. The hooks protrude through the skin and, when worked, the lure travels through the water with the hooks upright. The water should flow through the small hole so that it inflates the skin, which is turned inside out and has a light purple or blue look. When worked in a stop-and-go fashion, the skin jig looks like a small fish or even a live squid.

Some anglers fishing in New England also like to use an eel skin pulled over a metal squid and tied in front. Some metal squids are made with a ring around them to which the skin is attached. Still other surf anglers like to pull the eel skin over a large swimming plug. Here, of course, you have to remove the hooks first, pull on the skin, and then replace the hooks.

Rigged eels, eel bobs, and eel skins must be preserved in some kind of solution for future use. Most anglers make a heavy brine using coarse Kosher salt and store the eels and eel skins in the brine in jars or jugs.

But because natural eels and eel skins are often difficult to find, rig, and preserve, imitations of these lures have been sought. Two surf anglers, Al Reinfelder and Lou Palma, have come up with the Alou Eel, a plastic eel that has become an almost immediate success. The Alou Eels come in 9-, 10-, 12-, and 14-inch lengths and weigh from about 1 ounce to 3½ ounces. The most effective colors are the natural gray, amber, and eel-skin blue. The Garcia Corporation makes and distributes these eels. The Burke Fishing Lures Company also makes a plastic eel.

BAIT TAIL

ALOU EEL

The Bait Tail, a shorter version of the plastic eel, is really a plastic jig and uses a few inches of plastic eel tail attached to a lead head with a single hook. It comes in a variety of colors and sizes in weights from ¼ ounce to 3½ ounces.

The older, original jigs—called bullheads, bucktails, and bug-eyes—are also very good lures for surf fishing. They are available in various weights, colors, and hook sizes. The heavy lead head may be silver, white, yellow, or some other color. The skirts may be made of feathers, bucktail hair, plastic, or nylon. In recent years anglers have been effectively using these jigs with short plastic worm tails or special shrimp-type tails for many of the

JIGS

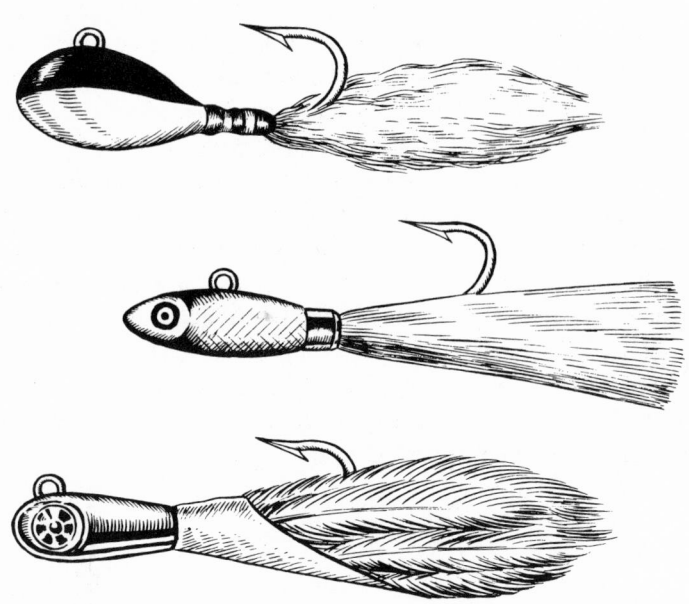

smaller fish found in the surf and especially for weakfish and sea trout. You can also add a strip of pork rind to the hook of the jig for extra appeal. Jigs weighing from about ½ ounce to 3 ounces are the best sizes for surf fishing. They are most effective when used from jetties, breakwaters, and rocky shores and in canals, inlets, and river mouths with deep water and strong tides and currents.

Surf anglers also use combination lures such as the splasher rig that uses a section of broomstick or dowel. This wood splasher can be anywhere from 2 to 5 inches long and of various diameters, depending on the weight you need. It has a screweye on each end or a wire running through the middle with eyes formed on each end. The fishing line is attached to one end and an 18- to 24-inch leader of mono is tied to the other. At the end of this leader you can tie a small streamer fly, feather, jig, or small spoon. The wood splasher provides casting weight for these small lures and when you reel or jerk the wood dowel it causes a surface commotion or splash which attracts fish. The lure itself trails just behind, a few inches below the surface. This combo rig is especially effective for school stripers, bluefish, pollock, and mackerel.

A somewhat similar idea is a large surface plug with a 6- to 8-inch dropper and strip of pork rind or a bucktail running about 2 feet ahead. In this double lure the plug acts as the attractor and weight for casting, while the smaller pork rind or bucktail travels just ahead and a few inches below the surface. Sometimes the fish will strike the plug, but more often they go for the smaller lure.

It's a good idea always to carry a jar or two of pork rind on surf fishing trips. The strips can be added to the hooks of plugs, metal squids, jigs, spoons, and other lures.

NATURAL BAITS

When artificial lures fail to lure fish in the surf the wise angler turns to natural baits. Many surf anglers look down on bait fishing or bait fishermen, but recently even these anglers have conceded that there are times when such live baits as eels catch more fish and bigger ones. And certain fish rarely take artificial lures so you have to resort to natural baits. Bait fishing in the surf is also a very relaxing form of fishing, less tiring than squidding with artificial lures. But the main reason for using natural baits is that there are many times when they are more productive than artificial lures. We'll cover the most popular baits used in the surf.

BLOODWORMS

Bloodworms are the round, smooth-bodied pink worms also known as white worms or beak throwers. They get the latter name because when handled they shoot out a long proboscis armed with four tiny black jaws or beaks. Two kinds of bloodworms are found along the Atlantic Coast from Canada to the Carolinas in tidal mud flats. They can be dug at low tide with a garden fork or clam rake or bought from bait and tackle dealers. A similar worm is found along the Pacific Coast, but it is not too plentiful, and bloodworms are flown from the East Coast to supply the demand there. In fact, bloodworms are dug in New England, mostly in Maine, and are shipped to many Southern states for surf fishing. Besides being used for whiting (kingfish), bloodworms also make good bait for blackfish or tautog, porgies or scup, flounders, and spot. Two or three whole bloodworms on a hook make a top bait for striped bass. On the Pacific Coast similar worms are used for croakers and surf perch.

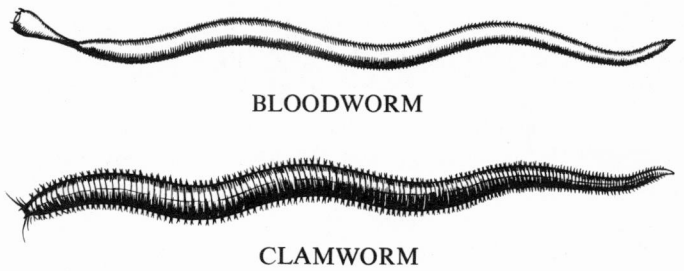

BLOODWORM

CLAMWORM

CLAMWORMS

Clamworms—or sandworms, as they are often called—differ from bloodworms in that they are flatter and have dark green or bluish backs and red or orange undersides. They also have visible segments and appendages or "legs" along their sides. Clamworms are often found on the same tidal flats as bloodworms but usually lie deeper in the mud and sand; you have to dig twice in the same spot to reach them. Clamworms are found along the Atlantic Coast from Canada to New Jersey. Along the Pacific Coast, where they are called mussel or pile worms, they are found from Alaska to San Diego. You can buy clamworms from bait or tackle dealers.

Along the Atlantic Coast you can use clamworms for weakfish, striped bass, flounders, blackfish or tautog, porgies, whiting, and other bottom species. Along the Pacific Coast they will take corbina, spotfin and yellowfin croakers, surf perch, and rockfish.

SURF CLAMS

The big surf or skimmer clam is a popular bait along the Atlantic Coast. The clams live in the sand along the beaches and to about 60 to 80 feet offshore. They dig into the sand and lie partly exposed. If you wade along the beaches in water up to a few feet deep you will often see them and can dig them out for bait. They are sometimes washed up on the beaches, especially after storms and heavy seas. Then you can pick them up at low tide. Surf clams are sold by many bait dealers and coastal tackle shops, and they can be kept on ice or in a cool spot for several days. The whole insides of a surf clam can be used for such fish as striped bass, channel bass, and black drum. Smaller pieces can be used for porgies, croakers, blackfish, and sea flounders.

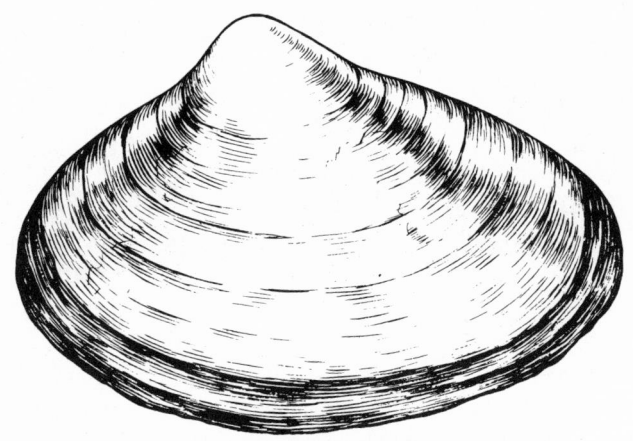

SURF CLAM

RAZOR AND JACKKNIFE CLAMS

Many species of long razor and jackknife clams are found along both the Atlantic and Pacific Coasts. They live in the sand and mud flats of bays and along ocean beaches where they lie buried beneath the surface. They can dig down fast and must be caught quickly, usually with special spears which are pushed into the hole the clams leave. Razor clams aren't used too often in surf fishing but they will take many of the same species which go for surf clams. The jackknife clam found along the Pacific Coast makes a good bait for spotfin and yellowfin croakers, rockfish, and corbina.

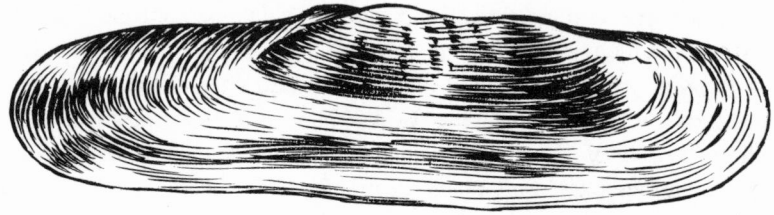

JACKKNIFE CLAM

MUSSEL

MUSSELS

Mussels are found along almost any ocean front clinging to rocks and piles and on mud flats and are easy to gather at low tide. These bivalves make good bait for many species found in the surf. Along the Atlantic Coast the edible mussel can be used for porgies, blackfish or tautog, and flounders. Along the Pacific Coast the big sea mussels can be used for spotfin croakers, corbina, cabezone, and rockfish.

BLUE CRABS

The blue crab is the bay crab found along most of the Atlantic Coast. It is sold in fish markets and served in restaurants. The soft-shelled and shedder stages of the blue crab make the best bait. Crabs molt, or shed their hard shells, to grow. A shedder or "peeler" crab has reached the stage where it is ready to cast off its hard shell, at which time it is a soft-shell crab. Both shedders and soft-shells can be used for bait. The soft-shell can be used as it is, but you must crack and remove the hard covering of a shedder before using it for bait.

Soft-shelled blue crabs are sold in fish markets, but they are expensive. Some bait dealers also carry shedders, and these also cost quite a bit. Thus most surf anglers catch their own crabs. This can best be done by wading in shallow bays among the

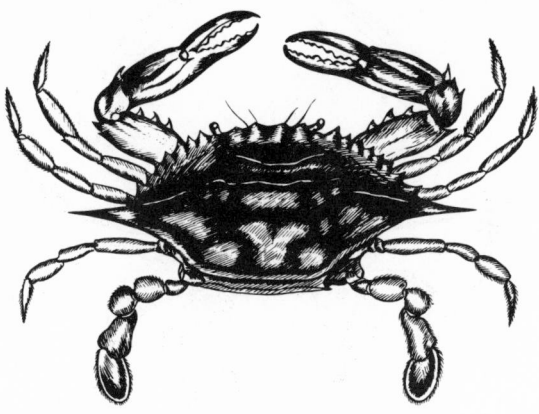

BLUE CRAB

eelgrass and sea lettuce and scooping the crabs up with a long-handled dip net. Hard-shelled crabs can also be caught in many kinds of traps. Crabs are kept in damp seaweed in a cool spot until they are used.

For striped bass, channel bass, black drum, tarpon or snook, use a whole soft-shell or shedder. Black drum and tarpon will often take a small hard-shell crab, too. For weakfish, sea trout, whiting or kingfish, croakers, and other small fish use a claw, leg, or section of the body of a soft-shell or shedder crab. You may have to tie the crab bait around a hook with thread if you are casting any distance so it won't fly off during the cast.

LADY CRABS

The other crab used in surf fishing is the lady crab, also called the calico crab or sand crab. It is found along sandy beaches from Cape Cod to the Gulf of Mexico. Lady crabs often steal baits from surf anglers fishing the bottom. These crabs also make excellent bait in the soft and shedder stages. Lady crabs can often be caught with the same long-handled nets used to catch blue crabs, or you can use an ordinary garden rake with a wire box at-

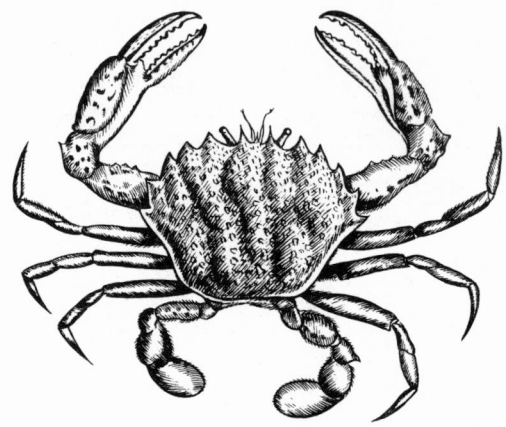

LADY CRAB

tached as a trap to catch the crabs as they are dug from the sand. The whole soft-shell or shedder crab makes a top-notch bait for striped bass, channel bass, black drum, weakfish, and bluefish. Pieces can be used for most of the smaller species that feed in the surf.

SAND BUG

SAND BUGS

Sand bugs are also called beach bugs, sand crabs, mole crabs, and sand fleas. They are, however, larger than the true sand fleas. Sand bugs are easily recognized by their oval-shaped bodies, which look like tiny, tan-colored eggs. They are smooth on top and have legs underneath with which they can bury themselves in the wet sand along the surf. They are most numerous where the waves curl over and break on the beach. They are found along both the Atlantic and Pacific Coast. You can catch them by probing with your hands in the wet sand as a wave recedes. To gather them in larger quantities use a scoop trap made of wire mesh. This has a long handle and it is dragged against the receding wave so that the sand bugs are washed into it.

Sand bugs can be kept alive in a cool spot for a few days. A Styrofoam cooler is good for this. When using them for bait put several on a hook for big fish and one or two for smaller fish. They make a great bait for pompano, tautog or blackfish, whiting or kingfish and can also be used for striped bass, channel bass, black drum, corbina, and spotfin and yellowfin croakers. For the smaller fish just run the hook through them once in from the underside and out through the back.

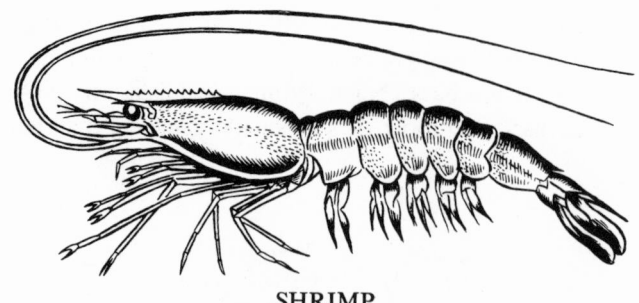

SHRIMP

SHRIMP

Many kinds of shrimp can be used for surf fishing, the most common being the jumbo or edible shrimp sold in most fish markets. Here you get just the tails with the meat and after peeling them you have a good bait for weakfish, channel bass, kingfish, and other fish found in the surf.

In warmer areas you can sometimes net live shrimp at night with a light. Or you can buy them from a bait dealer. These shrimp are usually a somewhat smaller species, and so they are usually used whole and alive on the hook. Shrimp are hooked through the back or tail and will catch weakfish or sea trout, channel bass or redfish, black drum, pompano, snook, and flounders.

Along the Pacific Coast surf fishermen use ghost shrimp or burrowing shrimp for bait. Three kinds of ghost shrimp live in the sandy mud of bays and estuaries. They can be dug with a shovel or spade. They are also sold in bait shops as salt-water crawfish. Ghost shrimp make good bait for surf perch, croakers, halibut, and other fish that come close to shore to feed.

MULLET

Mullet are a silvery baitfish often used in surf fishing, especially from the Carolinas south to Florida and along the Gulf of Mexico. However, they also migrate to northern waters and can be used there for many fish. Two kinds of mullet—the smaller silver mullet and the larger striped mullet—are generally found in the surf and make good bait. If you have a long seine, you can catch your own mullet by locating a school in shallow water near shore and encircling it.

A circular cast net thrown over a school of mullet can also be used to catch them. Mullet usually come closer to shore when they are chased by larger fish or at night, the best time to catch them. If they are thick you can often snag a few for bait by casting a lure or a treble hook rig into them and hooking them in the body. You can also buy mullet fresh or frozen in fish markets, or from bait dealers or tackle shops.

The smaller mullet can be used whole for such fish as striped bass, channel bass, bluefish, snook, weakfish, and sea trout. Larger mullet can be used whole for big tarpon or sharks. You can also cut the larger mullet into chunks or fillet them and use the sections for many of the fish listed above. Still smaller pieces can be used for many of the other surf fish and bottom species that feed in the surf or around jetties, piers, and rocky shores.

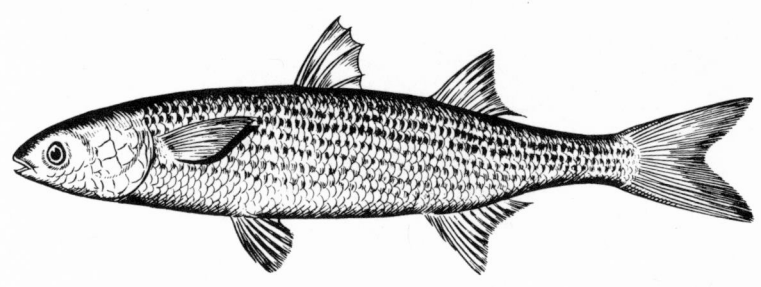

MULLET

MENHADEN

Menhaden is another fish commonly used by surf anglers. Often called the mossbunker, or "bunker" for short, it is an oily, flat, deep-bodied member of the herring family. Several species of menhaden are found in the Atlantic and the Gulf of Mexico. They are usually caught by commercial fishermen in purse seines. Surf anglers can buy fresh or frozen menhaden from bait dealers. Sometimes menhaden can be caught with haul seines or cast nets when they come close to shore. Or you can try snagging some bunker from a boat or jetty or shore by casting lures or treble bait-snatching rigs into them. They can then be used alive by casting them right out again to catch big striped bass or bluefish.

But most menhaden are used dead and small whole ones make a good bait for striped bass, bluefish, channel bass, and weakfish. A whole large menhaden makes one of the best baits for sharks. And you can also cut up large menhaden into chunks or fillets and strips and use them for many of the fish mentioned above.

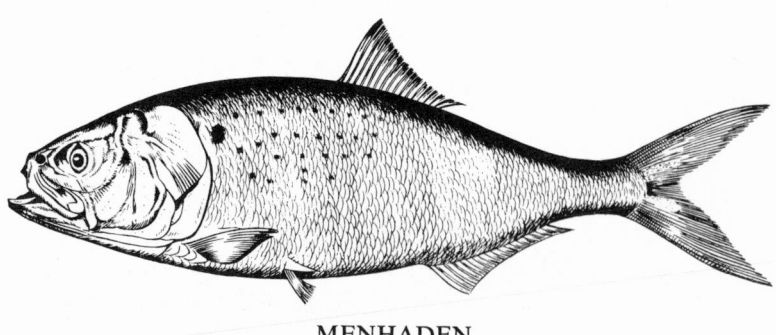

MENHADEN

EELS

The common eel has been used for bait in the surf for a long time, mostly on or near the bottom with a sinker or weight. You can use a whole eel either alive or dead, or you can cut one into sections and use them on a bottom rig.

Recently anglers have been using the eels alive by hooking them through the eyes, lips, or jaws and casting them from beaches, rocky shores, or jetties for big striped bass and bluefish. You can use the live eel on a plain line, or you can add a cork or plastic float a few feet above the hook. No sinker or weight is used; you simply cast the live eel into likely spots and let it swim around to attract fish. A live eel fished near the bottom with a sinker makes an excellent bait for sharks. And, as covered in the previous chapter, you can rig a dead eel and use it for a casting lure.

EEL

OTHER BAITFISH

Surf anglers also use many other baitfish depending on the location being fished and the species sought. Mackerel make good bait; use the smaller ones whole and cut the larger ones into chunks or strips. Live mackerel can also be used for big striped bass the same way you use live eels. Along the Atlantic Coast they will also catch bluefish, weakfish, channel bass, and other species. Along the Pacific Coast fresh and sugar-cured mackerel can be used for surf perch, spotfin and yellowfin croakers, and rockfish.

Anglers along the Pacific Coast also use herring to catch rockfish, ling cod, perch, and tomcod. When fishing from jetties around inlets, use live herring for salmon and striped bass. Another good West Coast bait is the smelt, which is caught in frame dip nets or snagged with hooks or lures when these fish run along the beaches. Sardines and anchovies can also be used for many fish.

Other baitfish include sand eels, spearing or silversides, killifish, and other small baitfish. Larger fish such as bonito, blue runners, porgies, jacks, spot, croakers, and whiting or kingfish can also be cut up and used as bait. A butterfish makes a good bait for striped bass or bluefish.

SQUIDS

The natural squid makes an effective and versatile bait for many surf fish. They are usually found in deeper waters offshore where they are caught commercially for food or bait. But in some places and at certain times of the year squid come close to shore, usually at night, and they can then be caught with dip nets or snagged with treble hooks baited with small fish. But most surf anglers buy their squid either fresh or frozen from bait dealers or fish markets.

A whole squid makes an excellent bait for big striped bass, channel bass, or big bluefish. Smaller squid or just the head or body can be used for weakfish, cod, pollock, and the smaller stripers and blues. Strips in various sizes can be used for small weakfish, summer flounder or fluke, porgies, sea bass, and whiting or kingfish. You can keep squid on ice or freeze them for future use, but many surf anglers prefer to cut them into strips and put them in a jar with heavy brine.

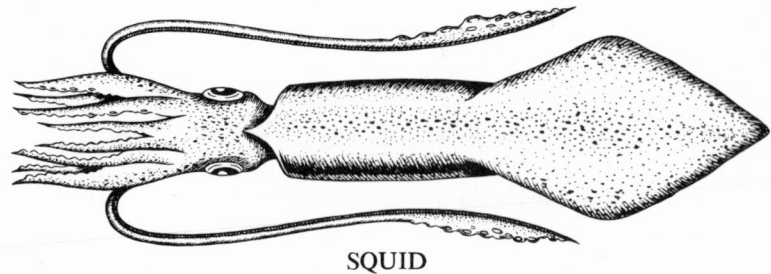

SQUID

BOTTOM RIGS

The surf angler who uses natural baits must know how to make up rigs for such fishing. By using the sinkers, snaps, swivels, hooks, and leader material described in Chapter 3, the surf angler can readily make up surf rigs for bottom fishing.

The basic surf fishing rig is the so-called standard surf rig, which uses a three-way swivel. The sinker is tied on a short dropper to one eye of the swivel, and the leader and hook are tied to another eye. This leader can be nylon monofilament, cable wire, or stainless-steel wire and can vary in length from 12 to 30 inches, depending on the fish being sought and the fishing being done. And, of course, you use the hook size and pattern best suited for the fish you want to catch. Finally the fishing line is tied to the remaining eye of the three-way swivel and the rig is ready to use.

The other rig often used in surf fishing is the fish finder. The fish finder with a ring on one end and a snap on the other for the sinker can be bought in any coastal tackle shop. The fishing line goes through the ring and a barrel swivel is tied to the end of the line. Then the leader with the hook is attached to the eye of the barrel swivel. The idea is to allow a suspicious fish to pick up the bait and move off with it for a short distance without dragging the sinker. The line just slides freely through the ring of the fish finder, or is supposed to. When you cast or retrieve this rig, the barrel swivel acts as a stop at the ring of the fish finder.

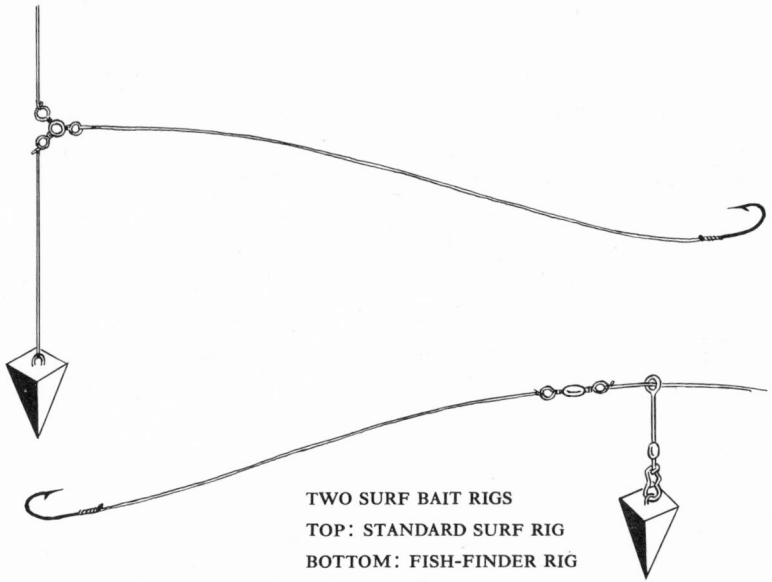

TWO SURF BAIT RIGS
TOP: STANDARD SURF RIG
BOTTOM: FISH-FINDER RIG

A similar rig often used in the surf or from piers or jetties in Florida uses an egg sinker with a hole in it. The fishing line goes through the hole and a barrel swivel is tied to the end of the line. Then the leader and hook are attached to the barrel swivel. This rig is better for fishing over rocky or coral bottoms because the egg sinker gets hung up less often than a pyramid sinker, which is usually used along sandy beaches with the two rigs described above.

Another good rig to use over rocky bottoms and from jetties and rocky shores is similar to the basic bottom rig or deep-sea rig used from boats. For this you tie a three-way swivel about 8 or 10 inches above a bank-type sinker. Then the 12- to 20-inch leader with the hook is tied to another eye of the swivel and the fishing line is tied to the remaining eye.

Along the Pacific Coast many surf anglers like to use a two-hook rig. In this a pyramid sinker is tied to the end of the line and one hook on a short leader is tied 18 to 20 inches above the weight. The second hook, on a shorter leader, is tied about 20 inches above the first hook. With this rig you can use one bait on the lower hook and another on the upper and so fish for two species at once.

Many variations of all these rigs can be made and used in surf fishing. You can easily learn which rigs are best in your area by watching the experts and studying their rigs. Or ask an experienced surf angler or your local tackle dealer to show you how to tie certain rigs for certain fish.

You'll find that you can save a lot of valuable fishing time by tying up some of these rigs and putting them, neatly coiled and ready for use, into marked envelopes. Then when you need a rig or lose one, just attach the sinker to the made-up rig and you are ready to go whenever the fish are feeding or the tide is right.

WIND, WEATHER, WATER, AND TIDES

It takes much more to be a successful surf angler than just having the right tackle, lures, and baits. A good surf angler is also a keen observer and student of winds, weather, water, tides, and the baitfish swimming in the surf. All these play an important part in whether fishing will be good on a given day.

Take winds, for example, and their effect on surf fishing. They have ruined more fishing trips than any other single factor, yet winds have also been responsible for some of the best surf fishing. This may sound contradictory, but the quality of fishing depends on the velocity and direction of the wind, time of year, water temperature, area being fished, and, of course, the type of waves encountered on a particular day.

Generally speaking, along the Atlantic Coast fairly strong winds from the east, northeast, south, southeast, and southwest create waves and moderate to heavy surf. North, northwest, and west winds, on the other hand, tend to flatten the surf.

During the late spring and summer the prevailing winds tend

to be from the south and southwest along the East Coast. A light wind from the south doesn't affect fishing too much; but if a south wind is strong, then it makes casting difficult and, if it blows for any length of time, it dirties the water with debris and seaweed, usually making surf fishing difficult or downright bad.

A light or moderate southwest wind along the Atlantic Coast often creates good fishing. The wind is usually brisk or strong enough to create white water along the beaches, on sand or rock bars, around rocks or boulders, and off rocky points and jetty ends and washes out a variety of food and baitfish. The first day or two of a southwest wind are usually the most productive. If it blows for several days or increases in velocity the fishing may slow down or stop.

A very strong southwest wind makes it difficult to cast and work a lure properly. You may get a belly in your line and miss many hits from fish. However, when some kind of baitfish, such as mullet, is present, the fishing is often excellent despite the strong wind. At such times the baitfish may be at your feet in the wash and gamefish may be chasing them, so a short cast will reach them.

When the wind blows out of the southeast, east, or northeast, the fishing may be good for the first day or two. These are storm winds along the northern Atlantic Coast and they usually bring rain. As the wind increases or keeps blowing, the waves get big and ground swells may be created. At such times you may find good fishing along certain rocky shores, mussel or rock bars, and in protected coves and inlets. Along sandy beaches the water will often get roiled or brown and dirty with seaweed. Then the fishing will fall off until the water clears. If the storm continues, the wind increases and the waves get too big, fishing may become almost impossible or even dangerous.

After a storm along the Atlantic Coast, the wind usually dies or shifts to the west, northwest, or north. This is the time you should head for the beach because some of the best surf fishing takes place when the ocean settles down and the water starts to clear. The fish are hungry, the baitfish are on the move again, and various crabs, worms, clams, and other marine creatures have been washed out of their hiding places and make easy pickings.

If the wind blows for any length of time from the west, northwest, or north it will calm the water and clear the water. These are offshore winds along the Atlantic Coast and they flatten the surf. At such times the surf fishing may slow down or stop completely. But there are exceptions, such as in the late fall when the water gets colder and the fish feed more heavily on baitfish. The lower temperature seems to make the fish hungrier and more active. At such times, the fish will often feed even if the water is clear and there is not too much surf. Offshore winds, if strong, tend to make the baitfish hug the shoreline in compact schools. This in turn attracts the larger gamefish which often come very close to the beaches then.

You'll often hear surf fishermen use such expressions as "white water," "bass water," "dirty water," "brown water," "champagne water," and "perfect conditions" to describe the condition of the surf. The terms "white water" and "bass water" are used to describe surf rough enough to create a foamy, white water along sandy or rocky shores. Striped bass fishing is usually better when there is plenty of white water, since they feed more actively and are easier to fool at this time.

"Dirty water" can ruin surf fishing for two or three days or even longer. When the water is dirty, debris, seaweed, straw, or suspended sand particles make it almost impossible to fish. On almost every cast the debris or seaweed gets caught on the line or lure. Fish usually do not strike under such conditions. "Brown water" due to suspended sand particles also stops or slows down the fishing. Slightly brown water or milky green water may create good fishing. Some of the best striped bass fishing I ever had was when the water was slightly discolored. Under these conditions the fish do not get a chance to examine the lure or see the leader or line and they strike more readily. They also seem to be hungrier because the water during the preceding days was too dirty for them to see the baitfish. So when it starts to clear enough for them to see the bait or lure, they hit with a vengeance.

Crystal-clear "calm water," or "champagne water," makes for difficult or poor fishing. As mentioned earlier, calm water is usually the result of an offshore wind or lack of wind for a few days.

But here again there are exceptions, such as night fishing, when baitfish are very thick, and fall fishing, when the water is cold. Most surf fish that feed on baitfish seem to sense that it is more difficult to catch them when the water is clear, so they feed little or not at all. They wait until nightfall or for a time when there is some surf or the water is rougher. Even if the fish are looking for food, they are harder to fool in clear water, and you tend to get short strikes and half-hearted strikes; the fish may also follow the lure and then shy away at the last moment.

"Perfect conditions"—plenty of white water, the right tide for the locality, abundant baitfish and gamefish—make for excellent surf fishing. However, there are always exceptions in surf fishing and many a time conditions seem perfect yet the fish aren't there or aren't hitting. Here timing is important. Even with perfect conditions the fish usually don't feed all day long or all night long. They generally feed in brief spurts and you have to be there at the right time. Even so, the odds are tipped in your favor under perfect conditions.

Tides also play an important part in surf fishing and most expert surf anglers study the tide tables for their area before going out. You'll often hear these anglers saying that they are going to "fish the tide" or catch a certain tide. Thus if they find that a certain inlet emptying into the ocean produces best during the last two hours of the outgoing tide and the start of the incoming tide, they try to get there when the tide is about half out and to fish until it turns. Another location may be best during the first two or three hours of the outgoing tide. Then the surf angler tries to get there at high-water slack and fishes the first half of the outgoing tide.

Of course, it takes time to learn a certain area so that you know which spots to fish at what stages of the tide. That is why it's a good idea to keep a record of your catches in a notebook and write down the tides (and other factors) that produce best at any given fishing spot. Or after fishing a certain spot for a long time, make a mental note of the best tide there.

But even when fishing a new area, some general rules can be applied. For example, most inlets and river mouths produce best during an outgoing tide, especially the last two or three hours. Baitfish move in and out with the tides, and when the current is strongest, during the last half of the outgoing tide, gamefish feed best.

When using artificial lures I prefer a low tide or a tide which has dropped for two or three hours. Then there is usually more white water, surf, and movement and stronger rips and currents. Baitfish may be around during high tide, but if the water is lifeless and there is little surf, the bigger fish usually don't bother them. However, when the tide drops enough for the incoming waves to break against rocks, jetties, and sand or rock bars, creating white water, the fish often start chasing the baitfish.

Of course, in many spots high tides are best. This is especially true of flat beaches, bars, holes, and coves where the water may be too shallow to permit the bigger fish to enter at low tide. So they have to wait until the water rises before they can move in to feed. Bait fishing on the bottom is often good around high water.

In most areas the change of tide is a good time to be out. There are high-water and low-water slack periods, and at these times surf fishing is often poor. But the minute the tide changes, the fish start feeding or hitting again. If this change or your favorite tide for a certain location occurs around dusk or daybreak or during the night, your chances of catching fish are even better.

So by studying the tides and fishing the tides you can be down at the beach at the best time and save yourself many hours of wasted effort. The smart surf angler doesn't squander his time or energy casting when the tide is not good for a certain area. He gets there when the tide is right and fishes hard, then quits or moves to a nearby area where the tide is right.

Food plays a big part in any kind of surf fishing. Food or bait in the surf will bring fish in quicker than any other single factor. Surf anglers are always on the lookout for baitfish because they know that, sooner or later, the small fish will attract the large fish. During the day watch for leaping baitfish and gamefish or wheeling and diving gulls and terns. Toward evening baitfish usually move in to shore to seek protection in the shallow water. The larger gamefish often follow them and so dusk, night, and daybreak are prime times for surf fishing.

But too much bait or food can be as bad as no bait. Then the fish may find it too easy to fill their stomachs to be interested in a single lure moving through the water. At such times your best bet is to wait until a big school of baitfish comes by and cast right into it, especially when you see fish swirling or breaking water.

Many surf anglers also study the phases of the moon since they are certain they affect fishing. It has been my experience that the moon does affect surf fishing considerably. Year in and year out, records show that some of the best surf fishing takes place around the new moon or the full moon. I always try to plan surf fishing trips to begin three days before a new moon or full moon and to continue until two or three days after it appears.

We can only guess just how the moon affects surf fishing, but some conclusions can be reached by logic. The moon, of course, has a strong influence on the tides and when this influence combines with the gravitational pull of the sun, we get the so-called spring tides, which occur around new and full moons. At these times tides are highest, currents are strongest, and waves are biggest.

So during the new moon and full moon such predatory gamefish as striped bass, bluefish, weakfish, tarpon, and snook come in to feed in the surf. The strong tides and currents and big waves toss around the baitfish or uncover crabs, clams, worms, and other food. During these periods the water is also rougher and whiter and ground swells are more common. If the water is not too dirty, which is often the case, surf fishing is likely to be good.

When the moon is full you can often have good night fishing. The strong light makes it easier for the gamefish to see the bait and lures and to find the baitfish. This is especially true during the fall, when such baitfish as mullet, menhaden, and herring are migrating along the coast. They often move on moonlit nights, and gamefish come in to chase them.

I personally don't care too much for a really bright moon shining on the water at night, especially when it is directly overhead or high in the sky. If it is near the horizon, behind clouds, or setting, the fishing is better. On dark nights when there is a lot of phosphorescence in the water to light your line and lure, fish tend to be scared away. Fishing on moonlit nights when this "fire in the water" is less visible is usually better.

You can also find good fishing on dark nights when there is no moon. Although baitfish tend to be less active at such times, gamefish often come inshore to feed. Surf fish can find a bait or see a lure on the darkest night and many a fine catch can be made then. But the two extremes—calm, flat water and very rough water—often result in poor fishing even at night. The prime time is from about an hour before daybreak until the sun gets high and then again about an hour before sundown until two or three hours after dark. If you fish these two periods year in and year out, you'll catch more fish in the surf than at any other time of day or night.

The weather itself affects the fishing mostly through the winds, as explained earlier in this chapter. But the amount of light and brightness also seems to play a part. Striped bass and other gamefish tend to avoid a bright sun or light and go into deeper water during the middle of the day. Especially when you use lures, surf fishing is usually poor during bright weather. Bait fishing may be better in the daytime if you can reach the deeper holes. Daytime fishing is also better in the north during the early spring and late fall, when the water is cold.

For most surf fishing cloudy or rainy days are generally better than bright sunny ones. And fish seem to feed better just before and right after a storm. Along the Atlantic Coast a northeaster or the start of a hurricane can trigger some fast action for such fish as striped bass, channel bass, bluefish, and snook. Naturally at this time there is rougher surf and more white water and the baitfish get tossed around. But on many an occasion I've had excellent fishing for stripers at night even when there was still no sign of the approaching storm and the water was calm and clear. Evidently the fish sense the approach of the storm by the change in barometric pressure and start feeding even if surf conditions aren't perfect.

It's a good idea to keep an eye peeled on the sky, check the weather reports and, at the first sign of an approaching storm or hurricane, head for the beach. Or go out right after a storm, when the wind shifts and the water starts to clear.

FISHING SAND BEACHES

Most surf fishing in the United States is done from the sand beaches that front the long Atlantic, Gulf, and Pacific coastlines. The problem of locating fish in the surf confronts both the novice and the expert angler. Before you can catch any fish, you must know where to go for them.

These days this problem is often solved for the surf angler with little or no effort on his part, because when there is a run of fish at a certain spot the local rod and gun or outdoor newswriter usually mentions the hot fishing. Of course, the information may be a day or two too late to do much good, but at least you can keep an eye on that spot and check to see if the fish have returned.

Then again, with more and more anglers fishing the surf, it is not unusual for one to locate fish and then spread the word to tackle dealers or friends. Soon you'll see the anglers lined up along the beach, all casting and some catching. The newly arrived surf angler joins in the lineup and can thank the earlier birds for getting him into fish.

Suppose, though, you don't read about a run of fish or don't see other anglers fishing. How do you go about locating fish along a sand beach on your own? The obvious way is to look for diving or wheeling gulls, terns, or other sea birds. Birds actively feeding on small baitfish are a good sign that the larger gamefish are under them. Of course, such activity is reliable only when schools of baitfish are around. If the fish are feeding deep on some other kind of food—crabs, for example—you won't see any birds. But it pays to cruise along roads parallel to the beach or to scout in a beach buggy watching for signs of bird activity or other anglers catching fish.

Even if birds are just sitting on the water, watch them. They may be merely resting and waiting for the gamefish to drive the baitfish to the surface again. If the birds are working some distance from shore, keep an eye on them. Often the baitfish and school of fish will work closer inshore to where you can reach them. Or wait until dusk when baitfish usually move inshore and the gamefish follow.

If there are no signs of birds feeding, study the water carefully to see whether there are any baitfish. Baitfish usually reveal their presence by the ripples or dark "patches" they create on the water, or you'll see them skip or leap out of the water. Often you'll see the gamefish swirling or breaking water as they pursue the baitfish.

One advantage the veteran surf angler has over the novice is his ability to "read" the water along sand beaches to find good fishing spots. Unless you have this know-how you will waste many precious hours casting and fishing in unproductive waters. Usually it takes months or even years to learn how to read the water.

How, then, can a beginner fishing an unfamiliar sand beach have any chance of catching a fish? Well, there is one method, although it does entail a lot of walking and casting. When you arrive at a new beach, cast two or three times in one spot. Then move down the beach about 50 feet and make two or three more casts, and so on down the beach. On many occasions I've covered two or three miles of beach using this method and often I've worked my way back, too. You can use one kind of lure—for instance, a metal squid—on the way down and then change to a plug or another lure on the way back.

If you want to cover the most water using this method, don't cast straight out into the ocean at each stop. Instead, make one cast to your left, the next one straight ahead, and the third to your right. This way your lure travels over different territory each time. Of course, if you get a hit or hook a fish you can stop and cast in that spot for several minutes before moving on to the next. If you see a particularly fishy-looking area or keep getting hits you can spend more time fishing it.

This method can also be used when two anglers are fishing together. Both start casting about 50 feet apart, then one passes the other and stops 50 feet down the line. After a few minutes the second angler passes the first one and stops 50 feet farther down the beach. This is kept up until the stretch of beach is fished.

Whenever surf anglers decide to separate, some sort of signaling system should be worked out in advance so that if one gets into fish or locates a school, he can contact the other man. At night a loud whistle or yell is good if you're close; otherwise, use a blinking light. During the day you can wave your arm or rod to call your buddy.

However, instead of casting haphazardly along a sand beach, you can save time and energy by concentrating on likely spots. There are many clues to the type of bottom, depth of the water, currents, wave action, food, and fish that may be found at a given spot. The color of the water, for example, is a good indication of depth. Dark blue, dark green, or green water indicates deep water, usually a hole, depression, slough, channel, or cut. Generally these spots harbor or trap food and baitfish and are prime fishing spots.

When you see light green or yellow-green water, you know the spot is shallow when the water is calm. When the water gets rough these shallow spots turn brown if the sand is stirred up, or foamy white. Such water is usually found over sand bars or flat beaches.

Surf fish will often venture into these spots to feed if there is enough water to cover them.

The action of the waves also provides a clue to the depth of the water and type of bottom. Waves breaking some distance from shore indicate a sand bar or gently sloping beach. Where they first curl and break indicates a dropoff and surf fish often feed here. In fact, it's always a good idea to cast your lure beyond the first line of breakers and reel it through the white water.

When big waves do not curl and break until they reach shore, it means that the beach slopes sharply with deep water close to shore. Crabs and sand bugs are washed out by the breaking waves and baitfish swim in the turbulence, trying to hide from the larger fish. Or smelt and grunion come right up on the beach to spawn. So you can often take fish here with short casts since the striped bass, bluefish, channel bass, and other surf fish come right up to the beach to feed. Along such sharply sloping beaches it's a good idea to work your lure right up to the sand because the fish will often follow it right into the wash and then hit it. It helps to keep your rod tip low so that the lure will have good action right to the end.

If you notice the waves curl and break, turn white, then stop foaming and pass quietly over a darker spot, it means there's a hole, pocket, slough, or trough inside an outer sand bar. These spots are favorite hangouts for striped bass, channel bass, weakfish, sea trout, whiting, or pompano. They lie in wait for baitfish, crabs, sand bugs, or other food to get washed out or into the deeper spot. An outer bar running parallel to the beach usually has a slough or trough on the inside, and one of the best spots for surf fish is where the sand bar drops off into the deeper water. The inner edge holds fish waiting for the food from the sand bar to be washed toward them, or larger fish pick off baitfish swimming along this edge. Cast your lure or bait on the sand bar and reel it into the deeper water of the trough.

Outer sand bars nearly always have some kind of break or cut through which the water enters and leaves. Such cuts or breaks are usually deeper than nearby water, the current is strong, and a rip is created outside. These breaks are located on both ends of a sand bar, on one end, or right through the middle. Crabs, sand bugs, clams, and baitfish get caught in the currents created by the rush of water coming out of the slough or trough. So, of course, gamefish come here to feed or use the breaks as thoroughfares to the deeper water inside the sand bar. Thus it always pays to spend some time fishing the breaks with either bait or lures.

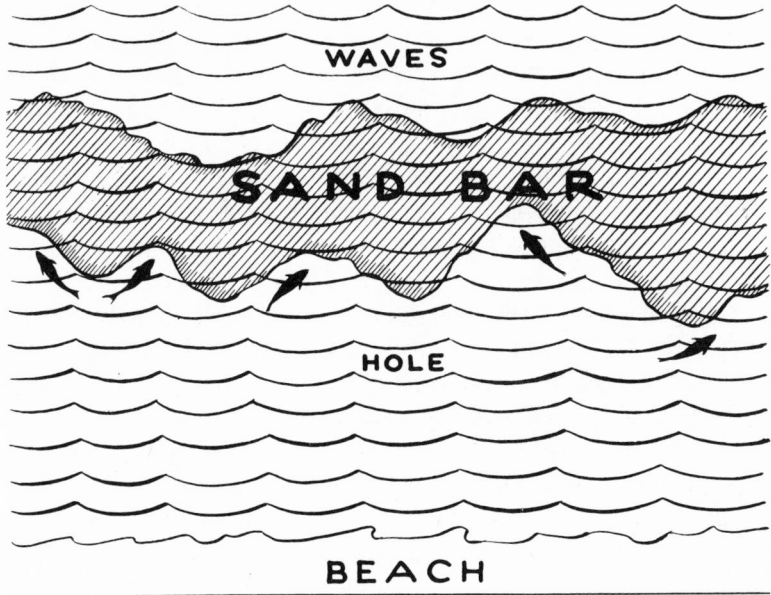

FISH LYING INSIDE SAND BAR

When the tide drops and gets near low, there may not be enough water on top of the sand bars and in the trough for good fishing. At such times it may be possible to wade through a shallow trough and get up on the sand bar to cast out into the deeper water on the other side.

Inlets or rivers emptying into the ocean along sandy beaches are always good surf fishing spots. There is usually a series of sand bars outside these inlets and rivers and plenty of white water and turbulence, especially when the tide is rushing out against the incoming waves. Inlets are good most of the year, but are especially productive in the spring and fall, when gamefish come out of the bays to feed on baitfish entering and leaving the inlets.

Beaches with many sand bars or an outer bar are good places to fish when the water is rough. The waves break on the bars, creating plenty of white water, then they lose some of their force in the shallow areas. On the other hand, when the water is calm look for a sharply sloping beach where there is deep water near shore. Here most of the wave action and any white water will be right up on the beach. Fish move in closer in this white water to feed.

You can often find the deeper holes, sloughs, troughs, breaks, and cuts along a sand bar by studying the shoreline from a cliff, sand dune, or hill. You can also see any gamefish or baitfish better from a high spot.

The angler who fishes sandy beaches must continually explore and study the shoreline. Sandy beaches are always changing because of shifting sands, erosion, wave action, currents, and storms. A section of beach that was poor last season may be hot this year. That sand bar which produced so many fish last fall may have disappeared by spring, or it may have shifted down the beach a couple of hundred yards. It pays to go down to the beach after every big storm or hard blow, and especially each spring after the winter storms are over, to study the shoreline and see what changes have taken place.

How you work your lures along a sand beach may mean the difference between fish and no fish. When using metal squids—or any lure, in fact—try to cast *behind* a breaking wave. Otherwise, an incoming wave will pick up your lure and bring it in faster than you can take up slack. A slack line stops the action of your lure, making it sink. And even if you do get a strike you won't be able to hook your fish.

However, when a wave breaks and rushes back to sea it creates a backwash and there is terrific resistance to your lure. Now you have to slow down your reeling or your lure will spin, revolve, and act unnaturally.

Generally a slow or medium retrieve is best with lures along sand beaches but for such fish as bluefish, bonito, albacore, Spanish mackerel, and other fast-swimming species a fast retrieve often produces best. When the water is calm and clear, fast reeling usually fools the fish more readily.

When using surface plugs such as poppers along a sand beach, keep them moving fairly fast at all times to cause plenty of commotion on the top of the water. You can pause, stop, or slow down for a brief moment, but you'll fool more fish if you make the lure splash and pop. If baitfish are moving along in the water, cast your plug beyond them and reel through them.

Underwater plugs should be reeled more slowly and you should feel them working at all times. When a wave moves the plug toward you, reel it a bit faster; when the wave recedes and pulls on the lure, slow down your reeling. You can try working any sinking or diving lure at different depths along a sandy beach. There are few obstructions to worry about and you can let the lure sink right to the bottom, then start retrieving it. That is where most of the fish will be anyway, either lying and resting or searching for food. Metal squids, heavy spoons and jigs, and rigged or plastic eels are especially suited for this kind of deep fishing.

Sand beaches also lend themselves well to bottom fishing with natural baits. Except for baitfish swimming on or near the surface, most of the food along a sand beach is found on or near the bottom, even buried in the sand. A crab, seaworm, clam, squid, cut fish, or whole fish cast into a likely hole, trough, or break will often produce when artificial lures fail. The best procedure when fishing a sand beach is to make a long cast and let the bait lie on the bottom in one spot for a few minutes. Then reel in slowly a few feet and let it lie in the new spot for a few more minutes. Continue doing this until your lure is at your feet. If you get poor results after fishing an hour or so, move down the beach and try another spot.

When you hook a fish along a sand beach you can let him run and play him freely, which you can't do fishing from rocky shores or even a jetty. Usually the fish will head out to sea or run parallel to the beach. You may have to follow a big fish down the beach a short distance. Your main trouble will usually come from other surf anglers fishing too close to you. When you're playing a big fish, you can yell to them to reel in their lines.

But the crucial period when landing a fish from a sand beach is when you are trying to bring him in through the wash. The waves are strong here and the backwash also pulls on the fish and strains your rod, line, and hooks. When the surf is rough, it may be a very tough job to bring in a fish, especially a big one, past the waves. You have to watch the waves carefully and respond to the pull on your rod and line at all times. When a wave breaks and washes up on the beach, reel fast to take up line. But when a wave recedes, let the fish go out again. Or if the strain on your tackle isn't too bad, you can try to hold the fish in one spot. Sometimes in rough water you may have to play a big fish back and forth in the breakers for several minutes before you can safely beach him.

Of course, another angler can help you beach a fish more quickly with a gaff, but unless he is cool and experienced he may lose the fish for you. When using light spinning tackle or light lines you need a gaff more than when using heavy conventional tackle. With patience and the helping waves you can beach the biggest fish in time.

If you do a lot of fishing along sand beaches in the wilder spots or less settled areas you'll find a beach buggy or coach camper a big help in reaching the best spots. These should have four-wheel drive to navigate the soft sand found along many of these beaches. Such vehicles not only save you a lot of walking but you can also rest, sleep, and even live in them while waiting for the right conditions and for the fish to show up.

FISHING
ROCKY SHORES

Although most surf fishing is done along sandy beaches, excellent fishing is to be found along rocky shores of the Atlantic Ocean in Maine, Massachusetts, Rhode Island, and New York and of the Pacific in Washington, Oregon, and parts of California. On the East Coast you'll find striped bass, bluefish, weakfish, mackerel, blackfish or tautog; on the West Coast, striped bass, many kinds of rockfish, surf perch, greenling, and ling cod.

Rocky shores have several advantages over sandy beaches. First, they attract and harbor such marine life as shellfish, crabs, worms, and small fish, and these in turn attract the larger fish. Second, you can fish high and dry in many spots and still be able to reach deep water with short casts. And finally rocky shores seldom change much, so good fishing spots will produce year after year. In fact, any veteran angler familiar with a rocky shoreline can show you a boulder, sunken rock, reef, hole, or small cove where thousands of fish have been, and continue to be, taken.

Naturally it takes quite a bit of fishing to locate these spots.

Usually the surf angler tries a few casts in likely-looking places along a rocky shore. If he catches a fish or gets some hits he makes a mental note and returns to these spots at a future date. After he visits a spot under varying tides, winds, and weather conditions and at different seasons, he has a good idea of the best time to fish there.

A beginner fishing a rocky shore, however, is at a disadvantage because he doesn't have this knowledge. If he uses the trial-and-error method, it may take him years to find all the good spots. Fortunately, rocky shores have certain similarities which can serve as a guide to locating good fishing spots quickly even in a strange area.

Along many rocky shores you'll find high cliffs bordering deep water. These may look perfect but are usually avoided by experienced surf anglers mainly because they may have to stand too high above the water. You can't work artificial lures effectively from too high an elevation and a fish has to be lifted too far even if you are lucky enough to hook one. With small species this may be practical, but if you hook a big fish you will usually lose him. Most surf anglers look for lower rocks where they can stand a few feet above the water when casting.

If high rocks or cliffs have sloping sides or slope toward the water in front, they can be fished in the lower sections. There is often a ledge along the front of high rocks where breaking waves crash, creating a fringe of white water. Stripers, which do not hit a lure too often in the deeper, clearer water some distance from shore in such spots, may dash into the white water to grab a baitfish or get other food washed out by the breaking waves. The best procedure, therefore, is to cast the lure out into the deeper water and then reel it back to shore through the white water. I have watched schools of small stripers following my lure in the deeper, clear water; then, as it was about to disappear in the white water one of them would grab it. The best technique here is to reel quite fast in the deeper, clearer water, then as the lure reaches the wash, slow down and try to imitate the weak motion of crippled baitfish having trouble swimming in the turbulence.

Fish the breaks, pockets, gullies, or indentations in the high rocks carefully. Here, if the water is deep enough to hold a striper or other fish you will often get a fast, rapid strike. The waves usually sweep in and then recede, creating a backwash that washes out food or tosses around baitfish, so stripers and other fish like to lie here and wait. Your lure should be cast out and reeled through such a gully or indentation along one side and then the other if it is wide, or if it is narrow, right through the middle.

The higher cliffs or rocks along the Atlantic Coast with deep water in front are also good for bluefish, weakfish, mackerel, bonito, albacore, and other fish that do not particularly care for rough surf. They can often be seen feeding on schools of baitfish migrating along the coast in the spring and fall.

Along the Pacific Coast high rocks make good fishing for yellowtail, roosterfish, halibut, barracuda, white sea bass, salmon, and other species that normally stay offshore or are caught from boats. At times they move in close to shore to chase baitfish or scrounge on the bottom for food.

High rocks are also good spots for bottom fishing with natural baits. Rocky shores are difficult to fish with sinkers since rigs are easily fouled and lost in the rocks or kelp. Especially risky is casting into shallow water when standing close to the water on the same level. Here the sinker quickly catches behind some rock or kelp and gets fouled. But from a higher elevation you can often drop your sinker and bait into some deep hole almost straight down or at only a slight angle and thus not get tangled as often. Here, too, it pays to use small cloth sacks filled with sand or pebbles as a sinker. If they get broken off it doesn't cost as much as losing a lead sinker. Another trick when fishing rocky areas is to rig up a heavy wood float and attach a hook and bait a couple of feet below it. When this is cast out the float keeps your hook and bait clear of the rocks or kelp.

Close to high cliffs and rocks you'll often find low rocky points jutting out into deeper water. These points are prime fishing spots since the waves crashing against them create white water in front. You can cover a lot of water by casting in an arc to your left and right and straight ahead from such a rocky point. Even at low water these are generally good spots to fish since you can often reach deep water from them.

A difficult spot to fish along rocky shores is where many rocks, boulders, and stones of varied sizes are scattered in profusion over a broad area. Here any sinking or underwater lure gets hung up in the shallow water and then you get hung up. However, the profusion of rocks makes for good fishing on many occasions, especially during and after a storm when big waves crashing in the shallow rocky area create a lot of white water. Striped bass like such conditions and come in to feed if any schools of baitfish are moving through or get trapped in such spots. A metal lure reeled fast through such water brings a hard strike. Surface plugs are also good in these shallow areas; the floating type are often easier to use. The best tides in shallow spots are usually from high water to about two or three hours down. But I have also taken fish during low tides by wading out as far as possible and casting into the deeper water along the dropoff.

Coves, both big and small, also produce fish along rocky shores. In fact, it is in such spots that some of the largest as well as many of the smaller fish are taken. The formations of the coves vary; some may have exposed rocks and boulders, others seem free of rocks and have more open water. This is often deceiving because most coves have some rocks underwater that provide holes and pockets often covered with kelp or seaweed where fish like to lie.

You can catch fish in the coves during the day especially when the water is rough. Particularly if there are barrier rocks or reefs at the entrance to the cove, it is a good spot to fish in a storm because the force of the waves is broken here and smaller fish often take shelter in the cove. The larger fish come in to feed on them. Coves are also very productive at night. Some of them have deep water even at low tide and can be fished then. Many other coves have shallow water and are more productive during high tides.

It may take quite a bit of hard fishing on several occasions to locate the submerged rocks and boulders in a cove. One way is to go out in a boat when the water is calm and clear and scan the bottom to pinpoint the rocks. If you do any skin-diving you can go below or swim with a mask and study the rock formations and locate the holes. Or you can try spotting and studying the cove from a high cliff, sand dune, or elevated rock if any are in the vicinity.

Most surf anglers locate such rocks and holes by watching the waves break or by casting sinking lures. When the lure touches or hangs up on a rock they remember the location and reel a bit faster the next time. And if you fish the area often you'll soon hook a fish or get strikes in certain spots. After catching a few fish or getting hits you know where to cast the next time. In fishing such coves it's a good idea to regard every bump or touch as a bona fide strike. Many of these will not be, but if you come back with your rod tip each time you will hook many fish that otherwise would have been missed.

Coves with exposed boulders, rocks, or reefs showing above the surface are easier to fish. Here striped bass will almost invariably lie just inside the rocks on the shore side in the white water created by waves crashing over the rocks or boulders. Generally it takes only one or two casts into a white-water patch to find out whether a fish is there. After you catch a striper or two from such a hide, you can often come back within a few hours or the next few days and take another fish or two from the same spot. Striped bass do not let a favored feeding station remain empty for long. New fish are always moving in to replace the ones that leave or are caught.

If you ever locate a school of stripers in one of these coves you will experience some fast fishing. Most of the time they will be the smaller school fish, but at times stripers up to 50 pounds may be present. However, big fish are often "loners" or travel in pairs and if you get one or two big ones from a cove you're doing well.

A rock or mussel bar often provides good fishing when there are

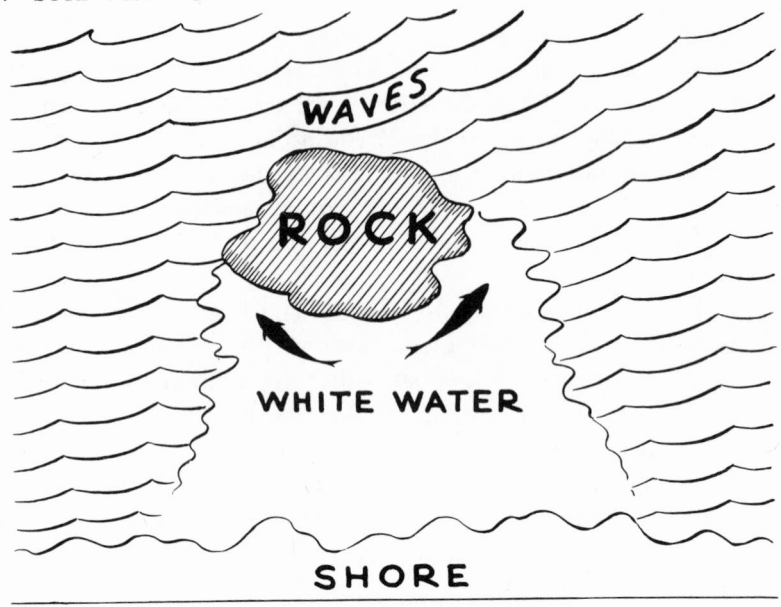

LOCATION OF FISH BEHIND ROCK

small round rocks or growths of mussels on the bottom extending and dropping off into deeper water. (Matunuck Beach in Rhode Island and the North Bar at Montauk Point, New York, are such spots.) Here the surf angler has to wade out into the water up to his hips and cast out in front of the bar or into any hole or dropoff in front. In such spots you may be fishing anywhere from 50 to 250 feet from shore.

Rock and mussel bars are usually good when the water is rough and baitfish take refuge in the shallow white water or have to swim through it. Use metal squids, Hopkins lures, and surface plugs or darters. Any sinking lure must be reeled fast, or it will get hung up. This often makes such spots tiring to fish, especially if you have to jump every time a big wave comes. But nice catches often result, and you'll need a 10-foot stringer to hold your fish since you can't waste time or lose your spot by walking back to shore every time you hook a fish.

Inlets and rivers entering the ocean are also excellent spots to fish along rocky shores. Here baitfish enter and leave and the current or rip at the mouth of the inlet or river sweeps the baitfish, crabs, and other foods to the waiting fish.

When fishing rocky shores you have to take certain precautions to fish them safely. Always wear a pair of wading sandals or ice-creepers over your boots or waders. The lower rocks are reached by the tide and are covered with seaweed, moss, or slime. A slip or fall can be dangerous. Avoid walking on wet, moss-covered rocks that slope at a sharp angle into the water. For better footing choose the more level, mussel- or barnacle-covered rocks. Watch the waves at all times to make sure you don't get hit unawares and swept out to sea.

Also, when fishing along rocky shores choose a spot where you don't have to do much climbing to land a fish. After you hook the fish, start working your way down to a low rock early in the fight. Then when the fish is licked you can manuever him into the landing spot and wait until the wave sweeps him high and dry if the rocks slope gradually into the water. In some spots you can work your fish between rocks into a crevice or shallow pool and then go down and pick him up. A gaff is usually not needed along rocky shores unless you have waded out some distance from land or are fishing from a high shore or rock where you can't go down to get the fish.

Rocky shores are not easy places to fish because you often have to do quite a bit of walking and climbing over rocks. Don't let anybody tell you that it isn't hard work, especially with a heavy pair of waders or boots on a hot day or night or when hauling a mess of small fish or a big fish or two over such rocks.

But I'd rather fish the surf along rocky shores than almost anywhere else. Each rocky point, cove, reef, bar, or cliff presents an individual problem that must be tackled and solved. You have to figure out where to cast, how to work your lure, how to avoid getting hung up, and how to fight and land your fish in a treacherous location, often with big waves threatening to wash you from your spot. This challenge makes for exciting and interesting fishing and I for one never get bored surf fishing along rocky shores. If I get tired of fishing one spot, I either move on to the next one to see what it has to offer or I hop into my car and drive down to another rocky area and try that.

FISHING JETTIES AND BREAKWATERS

To build homes, towns, cities, resorts, and beaches for bathing, man has leveled many of the sand dunes that acted as Nature's fortresses against the advancing sea. The result is that many of these structures are now threatened with destruction or flooding. Sand beaches are continually shrinking in size as the sand is washed out to sea, and inlets and channels used by boats or ships are always being filled in or changed. To combat the force of the sea and prevent erosion or at least slow it down, many jetties and breakwaters have been built along our coasts. These structures are especially numerous along the New Jersey coast and Long Island, New York. But all over the United States jetties and breakwaters have been built at most inlets, river mouths, and harbor entrances.

Jetties and breakwaters often provide good fishing, particularly for fish that normally hesitate to venture too close to shore. Almost every salt-water fish found in a given area can be caught from a jetty or breakwater at one time or another. Many of these rock piles have produced big fish. And when going after bottom species you'll find better fishing from the rocks than from a sandy beach. Jetties and breakwaters tend to change or even ruin the fishing from the nearby beach itself so a surf angler is forced out on them if he wants to catch fish in that spot.

Let's look at the bigger and longer breakwaters and jetties first to see how they can be fished effectively. These are the long, broad rock or concrete structures usually built at the entrances to inlets, rivers, or harbors to keep the channels open for boats. Some of them may run 2 miles or more out to sea. In some places, notably in Texas along the Gulf of Mexico, these jetties or breakwaters are often topped with concrete, making them flat and easy to walk on. Those constructed from granite boulders or rocks are also fairly flat when new, but as the years go by the rocks tend to fall apart or storms shift them and they sink or get covered with sand; walking on them then becomes more difficult and hazardous.

Most of the higher, broader breakwaters and long jetties remain fairly dry on top and do not get covered with moss except in spots where waves break over them often or where they are covered by the tide. Thus they are comparatively safe and comfortable fishing platforms.

As a general rule the long breakwaters and jetties found at inlets or river mouths have surf or ocean on one side and an inlet or bay on the other. At the shore end of the breakwater, you'll find some surf or breaking waves on the ocean side. This is a good spot to fish for striped bass, bluefish, channel bass, and whiting. During the fall, when mullet travel in big schools, you'll often find good fishing here since surf fish drive the small baitfish into the corner formed by the rocks and the beach. This spot is usually best when there is some surf and the water is fairly rough.

Moving along the breakwater toward deeper water you'll often find stripers feeding alongside the rocks, especially if breaking waves create some white water along the sides. As you move out on the breakwater and fish the deeper water you'll find bluefish, weakfish, pollock, mackerel, bonito, and false albacore in northern waters. In southern waters you can catch tarpon, snook, jack, Spanish mackerel, redfish or channel bass, and sea trout and such bottom feeders as croaker, spot, summer flounder, sheepshead, snapper, grouper, and jewfish feeding close to the rocks. Along the Pacific coast you'll catch rockfish, surf perch, ling cod, greenling, halibut, salmon, and flounder from breakwaters.

These and other species are often taken on both sides of a breakwater or jetty. Surf anglers fishing from the rocks with artificial lures usually wait until the fish show on top by breaking or until someone catches the first fish. But you can also fish blind by working along the breakwater and stopping to cast every 50 feet or so. In that way you can cover the entire breakwater. There is usually a good current or tide alongside the rocks and especially at the ocean end of the breakwater, where there may also be a rip that attracts the fish.

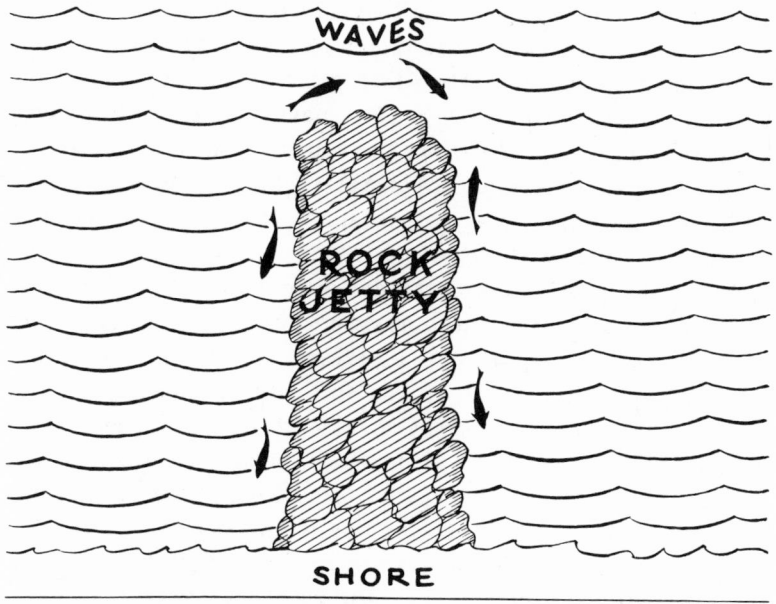

LOCATION OF FISH AROUND JETTY

When the gamefish are chasing baitfish on or near the surface you can use surface plugs, underwater plugs, and metal lures. If you use metal squids reel them fairly fast at first to keep them riding high where the fish are feeding. However, if the fish aren't showing or if they refuse to hit a shallow-running lure, let the lure sink deep and then work it back slowly with some rod action.

Fishing the shallow waters near shore from breakwaters and long jetties is usually best at dusk, daybreak, and during the night, especially when you're going after the larger gamefish. Later on when the sun gets high the fish may move out into deeper water and then you have to fish near the ocean end of the jetty or breakwater.

The shorter, smaller rock jetties that run anywhere from 100 feet to 200 or 300 feet are more numerous than the long breakwaters. They are found along many miles of beach, usually about a city block apart. When new, they are broad, high and fairly flat, making for easy walking. But they are usually built lower and narrower than the big breakwaters and soon break up as the rocks fall apart or sink. Then they get covered with slimy moss and the rocks tilt at various angles, making walking or climbing them difficult. These old jetties are tougher and more dangerous to fish, but most of them do produce at one time or another.

Rock jetties may also change somewhat each year because shifting sands may fill in one side and currents may wash out holes on the other. Sand bars are often found in front of the jetties. Thus a close watch is necessary to ascertain which jetties are best during a given year or season. Generally, however, if there is fairly deep water around the jetty on either side or in front, there is a good chance of taking fish. The higher, newer jetties can often be fished at high tide when the water isn't too rough, but the lower, older jetties are often covered at high tide and can be fished only when the tide is low or down quite a bit. On some of these jetties you can get out part way when the tide is about half out and you can fish the sides. When the tide is near low, the very end of the jetty is usually the best spot.

Most jetties have a strong current at the end and along the sides. Striped bass and other surf fish like to prowl or lie near such jetties. When the tide is near high and you can get out part way on a jetty you can cast from the sides. To cover the water more thoroughly you can cast in a semicircle—first toward the end of the jetty, then straight in front of you, and finally at an angle toward shore. After doing this a few times with the same or different lures you can go over to the other side of the jetty and do the same thing.

You'll find that most of your strikes from striped bass will come when your lure is near the jetty. Stripers like to follow a lure, and when it is caught in the wash and current created alongside the rocks or starts to disappear in the white water they hit it. Or stripers may lie in the white water breaking against the rocks right in close. For this reason it always pays to make a few casts toward the front of the jetty so that your lure travels close to the rocks, following a path like most mullet or baitfish when swimming alongside the rocks.

If the jetty is high or the tide is low, you can usually go out to the very end or tip. This is one of the best spots for most fish that feed in the surf because the water is deeper or you can reach the bars, holes, and troughs where baitfish and other foods are found. The currents and rips are stronger here and such baitfish as mullet like to hug the shoreline, but jetties act as barriers and force them to swim around the end. The larger fish know this and wait for the baitfish when they come around the front of the jetty.

One of the best ways to fish the end of a jetty is to "fan" it in a semicircle, making the first cast to your left, then the next one slightly to the right, and the next one still farther to the right and so on until you cover all the water in front of you. Some of your fish will be hooked way out, but here again stripers will often take the lure a short distance in front of the jetty. It is important to keep your lure working right up to the rocks.

If the rock jetties are in bad condition and you are forced to crawl out on them, it is tough work to fish more than one or two jetties during a favorable tide or period. However, if the jetties are short and fairly flat or new, then you can often fish several jetties in one tide or during the night. It's generally best to fish jetties at night since the beaches where they are usually built are crowded with bathers during the daytime. This is particularly true during the summer months or bathing season. In the fall or spring when the water is cool you can often fish during the day. But as with most surf fishing locations the best fishing takes place early in the morning, toward evening, and during the night.

One good system on the higher jetties or for any jetty during low tide is to start at the shore end on one side of the jetty and cast right into the wash or white water. After you have worked this spot, move up about 50 feet and fish there. Then move up another 50 feet and do the same. Keep doing this until you get to the end of the jetty and then "fan" it. After this you work your way back on the other side of the jetty, fishing it every 50 feet until you reach the beach.

Of course, after you have fished a certain jetty on several occasions, you'll get a fairly good idea of where most of the fish lie and where you get the most hits and you can concentrate your casts in those spots. Then go to the next jetty and follow the same procedure to learn that jetty's characteristics.

One bad feature about fishing the better jetties is that on weekends, holidays, and even on many weekdays they are often taken by other anglers. To fish the jetty properly, especially near the ocean end, there shouldn't be more than one or two anglers on any short jetty. You really can't work a small jetty the way you should if several anglers are on it standing close to each other. And, of course, you also have to watch out for flying lures or hooks. This is too much like pier or party-boat fishing and most veteran anglers shy away from crowded jetties and look for empty ones or fish late at night when the crowds thin out.

When fishing the longer breakwaters you can often take fish right in the channel, inlet, or river itself. Here the current is strong and the best lures are jigs, eel skins, or bait tails with lead heads that can be cast upcurrent and allowed to sink toward the bottom and then worked very slowly and as deeply as possible. In fact, bumping bottom every so often to make sure you are down deep enough is the best procedure. Such spots are usually best on an outgoing tide when the current is moving.

You can also fish from many jetties and breakwaters with live baits or even dead baits. To use live baits such as mackerel, bunker, herring, or eels walk out on the rocks until you can cast into deeper water. You'll catch big striped bass, bluefish, tarpon, snook, cobia, and salmon. Or you can put on a bottom rig to fish with natural baits. You can often fish a whole tide from a jetty or breakwater. When the tide is high you can cast the rig closer to the beach or shore. When the tide drops you can walk out on the rocks and cast into deeper water.

You can fish from wooden jetties along sand beaches if they are in good shape and you can walk out on them some distance. At one time such jetties were plentiful along the New York and New Jersey shorelines, but storms or waves have broken most of them and not many good ones remain. Even when in good shape such jetties are impossible to fish at high tide because the water covers them and you can't get out far enough. But when the tide drops you can often walk out and cast on both sides.

Striped bass like to lie and feed along the sides of wood jetties and will follow a lure and hit it close in. A good way to fish a wood jetty is to cast out toward the end of it and reel your lure alongside the structure.

As the tide drops, you'll often take more and bigger fish if you can get out toward the end of a wood jetty. There is usually a strong current right in front of the jetty and fish lie and feed here. And you can also reach many sand bars, holes, and troughs when out near the end of the jetty.

Wood jetties can be dangerous places to fish if the water is rough. A wave can come up, hit you hard, and knock you off. And the footing on the moss-covered wood is usually treacherous. Even when the water is calm you should fish wood jetties with ice-creepers or hobnailed soles that dig into the wood. Footing is usually better toward the end of a wood jetty if it is covered with mussels.

Landing a hooked fish from a wood jetty is also tricky until you have learned how by landing a few. When a fish is hooked, wait until it makes one or two long runs, then when it stops or turns, start slowly inching sideways on the jetty toward shore while fighting the fish. When you reach the area where the waves are breaking keep playing the fish in the wash. When the fish quits or turns over on its side, you can back up some more and then when in shallow water you can jump off the jetty and beach your fish.

When fishing from rock jetties or breakwaters bring along a long-handled gaff for landing fish. It's a good idea to fish with a buddy so that one of you can do the gaffing. If you do fish alone, place the gaff within easy grabbing reach. At night you need a headlight to follow the fish near the rocks and to see it when you are ready to gaff it. When the water is rough, take extra care so that a wave can't wash you off the jetty. All these problems and dangers offer a challenge and provide thrills which make surf fishing from jetties and breakwaters exciting.

ATLANTIC STRIPED BASS

The real "king of the surf" is the striped bass, especially along the Atlantic Coast from Maine to New Jersey. Because the striper grows big enough to give the surf angler something to brag about, the man who has caught a striped bass over 25 or 30 pounds has a worthwhile trophy. Yet he can always set his sights on a still bigger fish since stripers in the 50–60-pound class are occasionally taken from the beaches—and they reach even larger sizes.

Striped bass are also popular because they can usually be caught on some kind of artificial lure, they fight hard, and they make good eating. And they are a "smart" fish—very unpredictable, wary, and not too easy to hook or land. Most surf anglers would rather catch one striped bass, especially a big one, than a dozen other kinds of fish found in the same waters.

Unfortunately, striped bass are not too plentiful. Even during the years when they are most numerous they do not provide consistent fishing and they are always difficult to catch. If you see a surf angler who catches striped bass more often than other anglers you can be certain that he knows his stuff and is a hard, persevering fisherman.

Even the most successful surf anglers soon discover that fishing for striped bass is a "feast or famine" proposition. The surf angler will go for days or even weeks without catching even a single striper, then all of a sudden there's a "blitz" and he makes a killing. After that fishing slows down again with perhaps two, three, or more unproductive days, although it may pick up again later. This up-and-down pattern is, of course, due to the many factors discussed in Chapter 6.

Other factors, such as migrations and seasonal movements, also influence striped bass fishing. Striped bass are found along the Atlantic Coast from Canada to Florida and to a limited extent in the fresh or brackish waters leading into the Gulf of Mexico. However, they are mostly caught in the surf from Maine to the Carolinas. In other areas they are mostly bay, sound, or river fish.

On the Atlantic Coast there are local populations of striped bass that spend the winter in rivers and bays. There is also some spawning in these areas, so there is some surf fishing when the bass leave the inland waters in the spring and show up along the beaches. They return to the bays and rivers in the fall. But the biggest migration of striped bass takes place from the Chesapeake Bay region, which is believed to be the main spawning area for

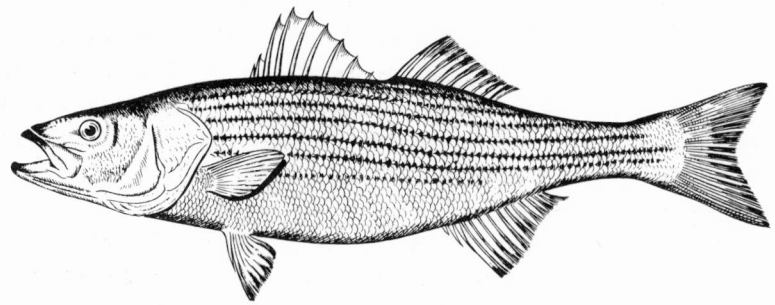

STRIPED BASS

striped bass along the Atlantic Coast. These fish head north in the spring and return south in the fall.

It's obvious then that if striped bass show up in large numbers in a certain area and stay there for a period of time, you'll have good fishing. Just why the stripers choose a certain spot and stay there is not definitely known, but a good guess is that water temperatures and food have a lot to do with it. If there are plenty of crabs, worms, or baitfish in a certain area stripers will naturally congregate there and feed as long as food is available. If food is scarce or the baitfish leave, the main body of stripers may follow them or move to other areas where food is more plentiful.

Of course, it's also true that there are always a few striped bass in almost every surf fishing spot where they are known to be caught, but these few fish rarely provide spectacular or sustained fishing. You need a good-sized school of stripers in a given area to provide even fair fishing. Even with thousands of striped bass along a beach and plenty of food for them, the fishing varies from day to day. Many times surf anglers are lined up casting their heads off and catching few if any stripers when some seiners come along with their nets and haul in a truckload. Striped bass seem to gorge themselves for a day or two or even a few days, then slow down or even fast for a few days. As mentioned earlier such factors as the weather, tides, waves, water conditions, food or bait in the water all trigger or stop feeding periods.

Seasonal migrations and feeding periods are important to the surf angler because they govern the fishing to be found at his favorite spot. As a general rule the first striped bass activity in the surf begins along the New Jersey beaches in early April, then extends to Long Island in late April. By May the striped bass are spread out along most of the coast and surf fishing is quite good on most Atlantic beaches, with the exception of the extreme northern areas of New England where the water is still cold. These first fish of the season are usually the smaller "school" stripers; by June they are joined by the bigger fish.

During the summer surf fishing for striped bass slows down in many places, but there may be exceptions in certain areas of New England such as Maine where the water stays cold and fishing is good even during July and August.

The peak striper fishing along the Atlantic Coast starts sometime in September and often continues until early November. As the water and weather cool, striped bass leave the bays, rivers, and sounds and school up along the beaches and rocky shores to feed heavily on the baitfish that have also concentrated in schools or, as in the case of the mullet, are migrating south.

When you hear those magic words "the mullet are in" get to the beach in a hurry. The first week or two of the mullet run are the most productive. Stripers of all sizes go wild at this time and you'll see them ripping into the schools of mullet as the small fish hug the shoreline and stay in shallow water to avoid them. The mullet can be seen rippling the surface or leaping out of the water. When they come to a jetty or rocky point, they swim around it, staying as close to the rocks or shore as they can. And mullet aren't afraid of white water or rough water—they actually seem to prefer it and seek it. No doubt they feel safer in the wash than they do in calmer, clearer, and deeper water.

The striped bass, however, follow them right into the breaking surf or take up positions around rocks and jetties or in holes and sloughs and wait for the mullet to come by. Then you'll see the stripers break and chase the baitfish. This, of course, makes it easier for the surf angler. He no longer has to look for the fish or cast long distances to reach them. Short casts will reach them and they are easier to fool in the white water.

At these times you'll get the best results if you wait until a school of mullet reaches the spot you are fishing before you make your cast. If you see a striper break water, cast into the circle left by the fish. Another trick is to stop casting when the water is calm and clear and then to cast as soon as a wave breaks over the spot where a fish was seen breaking or you think a striper may be lying.

When the mullet run is over or tapers off other baitfish may appear in the surf or the stripers may start feeding on small fish of various kinds. Striped bass are very adaptable and will eat almost anything that swims, moves, or crawls. They'll chase herring, menhaden, spearing or silversides, sand eels, whiting, mackerel, squid, and even bottom species such as flounder, bergall, and blackfish.

When stripers are chasing baitfish such as mullet or menhaden that tend to swim at the surface, they look for them there, so at these times one of the best lures is a surface plug—a popper, swimmer, flaptail, or similar lure that makes a commotion, splash, or ripple on the surface of the water. You can also use a darter-type plug. Originally made for fresh-water black bass fishing, then used in salt water for snook and tarpon, it is now available in larger sizes for striped bass. When reeled slowly or twitched, especially at night, it creates a slight ripple or wake on the surface. When reeled fast it travels just below the surface in a zigzag darting fashion like a terrified baitfish. Some fine darters for surf fishing are made by Stan Gibbs and a few other companies.

The stripers will also hit underwater plugs when chasing baitfish; the plugs can be retrieved at various depths. They work very well when the water is fairly rough and are good to use in strong tides, currents, and rips. Such plugs as the Creek Chub Pikies, the Rebel, the Rapala, and the Mirro-lure are favorites for striped bass.

When the water is very rough or you have to cast far into a wind to reach fish feeding way out, a metal squid or spoon-type lure such as the Hopkins or Kastmaster are good to use. Metal lures are especially effective when fishing for the smaller school stripers in early spring and late fall.

When striped bass are feeding on mullet, bunker, herring, or other large fish they'll also take a rigged eel or a plastic eel. These lures are usually used at dusk, during the night, and at daybreak when, I believe, a striped bass doesn't see the shape or size of the lure clearly enough to recognize it as an eel. Because of the bait-fish present, he mistakes the eel for a mullet, bunker, or something else. At any rate, some of the biggest stripers are caught on rigged or plastic eels.

If you really want big stripers in the surf, try using live baits such as mackerel, herring, bunker, mullet, or eels. These baits, of course, have to be obtained beforehand and kept in a small container to be taken to the fishing spot. Sometimes you can catch a mackerel or herring with a lure or snag a mullet or bunker or other bait with a lure or treble hook then put it on the hook of your fishing line right at the fishing spot.

Live baits can be used from a sandy beach, especially one which drops off sharply into deeper water or has a slough or trough where fish come in close to shore. But they are even better for use from jetties, breakwaters, and rocky points where you can cast into deeper water or the best spots which are close by.

One of the easiest and deadliest live baits you can use is an eel. You can put a dozen eels in a small pail and take it down to the beach and without any fuss or bother they'll stay alive for a long time. Hook a live eel through the eyes, lips, or side of the jaw, then cast it into likely spots or let the current or tide take it out into an inlet or river mouth. Where the water is shallow you can add a cork or plastic float about 3 or 4 feet above the eel. You can let it swim around naturally or you can slowly reel it in.

When you feel a striper grab it, give some slack line or wait several seconds before you set the hook.

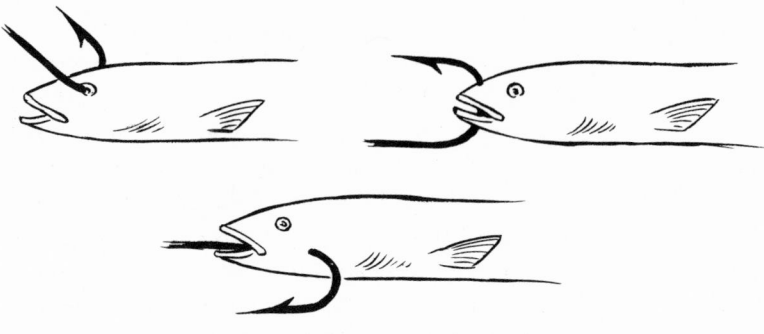

THREE WAYS TO HOOK A LIVE EEL

Striped bass of all sizes are also caught on natural baits by fishing on the bottom with a sinker. Sandworms and bloodworms can be used the year round and are especially good in the spring, when stripers are still sluggish in the cold water. Or you can try a whole skimmer clam, a small squid, or a squid head. During the summer and early fall a top bait is a soft-shell or shedder crab. You can use a regular blue crab, but a lady or calico crab, found along the sand beaches, is even better. Stripers will also take whole or cut fish baits such as mullet, bunker, herring, sardine, anchovy, butterfish, or mackerel.

The most successful bass fishermen put in a lot of time fishing. They go out as often as possible—at least every weekend —and keep in touch with the latest information on local striped bass runs. Newspapers often print such items in their outdoor columns but this is usually a day or two too late. For best results you should get down to the beach and check for yourself—talk to other anglers, swap information with a surf fishing friend, and ask the local tackle dealer about the latest striper runs and catches.

When you hear about a striped bass run along a nearby beach or shore it pays to get there as soon as possible. Holding off or waiting a day or two may make you too late—conditions will change, the stripers will stop feeding or move off, and then you will have to wait until the next run. The timing of your fishing trips is one of the real secrets in catching stripers in the surf.

Even if there is a run of striped bass along a certain beach it doesn't mean that the fish will feed all day or even all night. Stripers move in close to shore within reach of the surf angler only for short periods. At least, they feed or hit only for short periods—most of the time they are out in deeper water or resting on the bottom and not actively feeding. I've seen a few days when the fish hit for longer periods, say a few hours or a whole tide, but these occasions have been rare and most of the striped bass feeding in the surf is done in brief flurries. You have to be there then to take advantage of it.

The real striper specialists put in many hours on the beach so that they can be there at the right time. You'll see them along the beaches of Cape Cod, parts of Rhode Island, Long Island, New Jersey, and North Carolina camped in beach buggies, campers, trailers, or mobile homes for a whole weekend or days at a time waiting for the best fishing periods.

The peak fishing periods for striped bass are normally about an hour before sundown until about midnight or a bit later. Then there is usually a lull until about an hour before daybreak, when the fish start feeding or hitting again. Stripers will often continue to feed after dawn for two or three hours, until the sun gets too bright and high in the sky. If the day is cloudy, the water is rough, or a storm is blowing, the fishing may continue during the day, especially for the smaller school stripers. They'll also feed more during the day in early spring and late fall.

If you really want to catch a great many big stripers you'll do better if you fish at sundown, during the night, and at daybreak. Many anglers who have achieved a reputation for catching big stripers do all or most of their fishing then. Many of them fish all night from dusk to dawn and catch up on their sleep during the day.

One of the main reasons many surf anglers do not catch striped bass is that they fish when they feel like it instead of when the fish feel like hitting or feeding. I've had such anglers come to me and say, "I've been at this surf fishing for five (or more) years and I've yet to catch my first striped bass." Or they complain because they catch only small stripers and never a big one. When I asked these men when they go surf fishing, they almost invariably tell me that they get down to the beach around 7 or 8 o'clock in the morning, fish through the middle of the day and then quit around 3 or 4 o'clock in the afternoon. No wonder they don't catch striped bass—they're fishing too late in the morning and quitting too early in the afternoon or evening.

PACIFIC STRIPED BASS

Until 1879 there were no striped bass in the Pacific Ocean. In that year S. R. Throckmorton, chairman of the California State Fish Commission, thought it would be a good idea to introduce the Eastern striper to Pacific waters. He discussed the idea with Livingston Stone of the United States Fish Commission, who agreed that the project would be worth a try.

So Stone took 135 stripers about 3 inches long from the Navesink River in New Jersey. They were put into wooden tanks on a railroad car and the seven-day-long trip began. There were many problems along the way—maintaining the proper temperature of the water with ice, aerating the water with dippers at regular intervals, and adding sea salt to the fresh water to make it brackish. Even so some of the stripers were lost when the weather and water turned cold one night. On June 19, 1879, a total of 110 healthy stripers were released in the Carquinez Strait at Martinez near San Francisco.

In 1882 another 400 striped bass, 5½ to 9 inches long, were taken from the Shrewsbury River in New Jersey and shipped across the continent in milk cans. Some died en route, but 308 stripers arrived in California in fine condition and were released in lower Suisan Bay on July 24, 1882.

The introductions of striped bass to the Pacific turned out to be one of the most successful transplants of salt-water fish ever made. The young stripers found the water, climate, and abundance of food to their liking and grew rapidly and multiplied quickly. In 1883, 4 years after the first shipment, a 17-pound striper was caught. And in 1889, only 10 years after the first introduction, a 45-pounder was taken and large numbers of striped bass were caught for market. And in another 10 years the commercial catch of striped bass reached 1,234,320 pounds a year!

Sportsmen soon discovered the stripers, too, and started fishing for them with rod and reel, mostly in the bay, river, and delta areas near San Francisco. This was mostly boat and shore fishing in the quieter inland waters. When the first stripers appeared along the beaches near Golden Gate, surf anglers started to fish for them there. And in 1899 the first West Coast striped bass fishing club was established in San Francisco.

As the commercial catches of striped bass increased, sportsmen became alarmed and in 1926 they took steps to protect the popular fish. In 1935 they succeeded in having a law passed making the striped bass a gamefish. Now you can keep only three striped bass a day and they have to be more than 16 inches in length. You also need a salt-water fishing license in California to catch striped bass or any other salt-water fish. For many years striped bass couldn't be caught at night in California, but this law was changed not too long ago.

After the turn of the century striped bass started to migrate to a limited extent along the Pacific Coast and showed up in Oregon and as far north as the Columbia River. By 1925 they were firmly established in the Coos Bay region of Oregon.

Attempts were also made to extend the range of the striped bass by planting several thousand over a period of years in southern California, but stripers have not become very plentiful in those waters.

Evidently the striped bass along the Pacific Coast rarely migrate up and down the coastline in the big schools commonly seen along the Atlantic Coast. Most of the striped bass seem to be confined to the inland bays, rivers, and deltas in two major areas —near San Francisco, California, and Coos Bay, Oregon. Of course, Pacific stripers do leave the inland waters and feed in the open ocean and along the beaches, especially during the summer months, but they rarely venture too far along the coast.

The migrations and movements of the Pacific striped bass are not as well understood or charted as those of the Atlantic striper. Tagging programs have been started and studies are being made to learn more about the seasonal migrations and range of the Pacific striped bass, so in time more information may be available.

At present it is known that striped bass spend the winter in the delta and the bays around San Francisco, then in the spring start moving upstream into fresh water to spawn during April, May, and June. The most important spawning areas are the San Joaquin River, the mouth of the Middle River, and the Sacramento and Feather Rivers. After spawning, the larger bass leave the rivers and the delta and drop down to Carquinez Strait, San Pablo Bay, and San Francisco Bay. Fishing is good in those areas during the summer and fall months.

Most of the stripers seem to spend the entire summer and fall in these inland waters. In certain years, however, some schools of fish leave these inland waters and move into the ocean to feed on schools of smelt and anchovies. When this happens there is good surf fishing along the beaches to the south, usually beginning about the middle of June and often lasting into August.

But these beach feeding periods are irregular. The stripers may show up dependably for many years and then fail to show up for a few years. There were good surf runs from 1930 to 1965, then in 1966 the stripers did not come in any numbers and for the next six years surf fishing was poor. The fish returned in 1972, but how long they will keep coming back no one can say. Biologists who have studied these migrations believe that striped bass move out into the ocean in the greatest numbers during the years when the water is warm. They also believe that the fishing is better along the beaches in years when striped bass are plentiful. Or it may be that not enough smelt, anchovy, herring, or other baitfish are showing up along the beaches to attract any numbers of striped bass.

Whatever the reason, it will take more tagging and research to find out why stripers appear in big schools during certain years along California beaches and stay away during other years. In the meantime the surf angler should keep informed and take advantage of any runs that do take place. Fortunately this is fairly easy in the San Francisco area because the local outdoor writers, broadcasters, and tackle shops quickly let anglers know if the stripers are running along any of the beaches.

And you can't miss the runs if you go down to nearby beaches such as Baker's Beach, Ocean Beach, Sharp's Park, Salada Beach, and Pacifica. Here you'll see hundreds if not thousands of surf anglers lining the beaches shoulder to shoulder and, if the stripers are running, most of them will be pulling in fish.

If there are no surf anglers around, you can try to locate feeding fish by watching for gulls, sheerwaters, pelicans, or cormorants wheeling and diving into the water. The fishing is usually best when smelt come into the wash to spawn and the stripers follow them. This may happen two or three times a day, but these feeding sprees generally last less than a half hour. So you have to be there during one of these so-called bass busts to take advantage of the fast and furious fishing. During such periods as many as 200 or 300 stripers may be taken by the anglers on a short stretch of beach. These fish are caught on such artificial lures as metal squids, spoons, and plugs.

You can often see the stripers breaking water well off the beach or even close to the beach when they chase the baitfish. Many surf anglers like to go up on a high cliff or rock and scan the water and beaches with binoculars to locate the feeding schools.

Between these bass busts you can still catch striped bass when there is no surface activity by casting from the rocks located between the sand beaches. Unfortunately, not many of these rocky points or clumps can be fished. They are too high, too low, or too rugged and dangerous to climb; the rough surf breaking against the rocks also makes for tricky fishing. But if you can get out safely and cast into the deeper water you can often catch striped bass on surface and underwater plugs and other lures.

In fact, even during seasons when stripers are scarce along the beaches or the big runs fail to materialize surf anglers working the rocky areas have made good catches. It's just a question of waiting for the right tide, time of day, water conditions, and baitfish to trigger some action. As in most striper fishing, rough water seems to produce more strikes and better fishing than calm water. Night fishing on moonlit nights or dark nights can also be good along these rocky shores. Then slow-moving underwater plugs that ride just below the surface are very effective. And on dark nights luminous plugs often produce better than lures which do not give off phosphorescence.

Striped bass have been caught along the beaches and rocky shores in northern California and Oregon. Here again, the best fishing usually takes place when you actually see stripers chasing or feeding on anchovy, smelt, herring, or other baitfish. But you can also cast blind to likely spots and occasionally pick up a striper or two in the sloughs, troughs, or holes and around rocks, boulders, and sand bars at river mouths and inlets. Stripers will come into such places to feed on crabs, clams, seaworms, and sand bugs.

For Pacific stripers you can use many of the surf fishing rods, reels, and lines described in Chapter 2. Most Pacific Coast anglers prefer the longer surf spinning rods, from 11 to 14 feet in length, with the large surf spinning reels holding monofilament line testing 20 to 25 pounds. Conventional rods and reels are also used, and these too are long and fairly heavy in action. The reason for the long, fairly heavy rods is that the Pacific surf is often rough and the waves are high, so you have to make long casts to get out beyond them. And the lures and sinkers are often heavy, necessitating a sturdy rod.

You can use many of the lures detailed in Chapter 4. The most popular are the heavy keel-type chrome metal squids or the heavy, flat, hammered-spoon lures such as the Hopkins. Some of these weigh up to 3 or 4 ounces. The treble hooks on some of these lures may be changed to strong single hooks and some of these adorned with bucktail or feathers.

Various plugs can also be used along the Pacific coast; the surface poppers, underwater swimmers, and sinking models are the most effective. Plugs are usually favored on days when stripers come close to shore to feed, when you are fishing from rocky points or rocky shores where fish move in close, and when you are fishing at night.

When using such underwater lures as metal squids you can often catch fish when reeling the lures close to the surface. But you'll often catch more fish or bigger fish if you let the squids sink almost to the bottom and then reel them back.

On the days when stripers aren't chasing baitfish or feeding on top you can often catch them with bait on the bottom. Fishing with lures in the surf is relatively new along the Pacific Coast. For many years surf anglers there insisted that their stripers wouldn't hit or even look at artificials in the surf. So they continued to fish with bait until the big runs of stripers started along the beaches and anglers who used lures made big catches.

Now bait fishing has almost died out and most surf anglers prefer to wait until the stripers start running along the beaches and hitting lures before they go out. But you can miss out on some good fishing if you stick to lures and you also shorten your fishing season. Striped bass of all sizes will still take natural baits in the Pacific surf and you'll often catch the bigger fish this way—and you'll catch them from March to November.

To catch striped bass on bait you can use the regular surf bottom and fish-finder rigs illustrated and described in Chapter 5. Pacific Coast anglers often use a two-hook rig and 6–8-ounce pyramid sinkers for bait fishing, especially if the surf is rough or long casts are required.

The top bait for Pacific stripers is a sardine. If it's not too big, cut it in half and impale the head section on the big 7/0 or 8/0 single hook. Bigger sardines can be cut into chunks and used on a single hook. If you can get fresh anchovies you can put three or four on a hook by running it through their eyes. You can also try clams, seaworms, sand bugs, and shrimp.

A 45-pound striped bass was caught on sardine bait in the surf at Pacifica, but such big bass are not commonly caught along West Coast beaches. Most of the surf-caught stripers will range from a few pounds to 20 or 30 pounds. However, much bigger fish have been caught in the bays, rivers, and deltas. Many big ones up to 64 pounds have been caught in the Russian and Umpqua rivers. Way back in 1926 a record 72-pound striper was taken on rod and reel in the Russian River. And a 87½-pounder was taken in Suisan Bay in a net. So Pacific stripers do reach a big size and one of these days some lucky (or skillful) surf angler will catch one of these lunkers from the beach.

CHANNEL BASS

If the striped bass is the king of the northern surf, the channel bass is the king of the southern surf, especially from Virginia to Florida and along the Gulf of Mexico. Early in this century big channel bass used to come up as far north as New Jersey and a few stragglers were even caught along the Rockaways on Long Island, New York; but today such catches are rare and if you want good channel bass fishing in the surf you have to go at least as far south as Virginia.

The channel bass has many other names—drum, red drum,

redfish, red horse, bull redfish, red bass, bar bass, and spottail, the last being derived from the black spot at the base of the tail. Usually, there is only one spot on each side, but some fish may have as many as 23 small spots on one side. The channel bass is not actually red, but more of a coppery color which is dark red-brown in the larger fish and pink or pale brown in the younger specimens; the fish have silvery sides and white bellies. Nor is the channel bass a true bass. It is actually a member of the croaker family, which includes the drums and weakfishes. Nevertheless, it looks somewhat like a bass in general body shape. The name "channel bass" is used mostly in the north, in southern waters the fish is better known as the redfish or just plain red.

Whatever its name, the channel bass is highly prized for its fighting power and large size. It is one of the few large gamefish that can frequently be caught from the beaches. The other fish caught in the surf usually run small, but both the channel bass and the striped bass come big and give the surf angler a real workout.

Most of the channel bass caught along their northern range run from 15 to 40 pounds, but each year fish in the 50-pound and even 60-pound class are caught from the beaches, especially in Virginia and North Carolina. They have been taken in the surf up to 75 pounds, and even larger ones have been caught from boats and piers. Elvin Hooper caught a 90-pound channel bass from the pier at Rodanthe, North Carolina, on November 7, 1973. Farther south the smaller so-called puppy drum are more plentiful and if you catch anything over 30 pounds you have a big one.

When fishing for medium and big channel bass you can use many of the surf rods and reels used for big striped bass. Use the longer, heavier rods when fishing the beaches of Virginia and North Carolina in the spring and fall, when big channel bass are running. Spinning rods from 10 to 14 feet are popular. The largest surf spinning reels hold plenty of 20- to 25-pound-test line. You have to remember that most of the time you'll be casting heavy sinkers and big baits long distances and will need a rod with

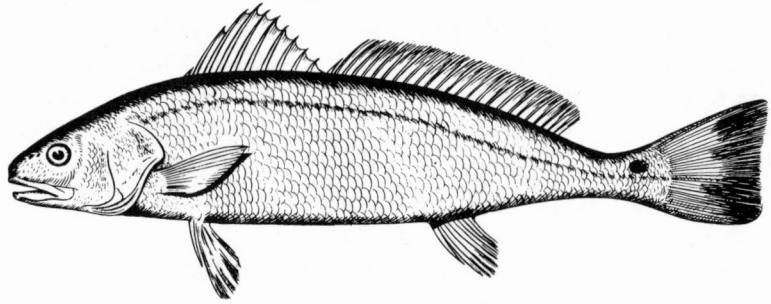

CHANNEL BASS

plenty of backbone to do the job. For this reason many old-time channel bass experts still prefer the conventional 9–12-foot rod and a conventional surf reel filled with 30–36-pound-test mono or braided line. You not only have to handle heavy sinkers and big baits and cast long distances, but on many days you also have to play big channel bass in rough surf.

If you do your fishing in Florida or along the Gulf of Mexico, you can often use shorter, lighter rods and lighter lines since the surf there is not so rough and the fish run smaller. You can use lighter sinkers and smaller baits, too. In fact, many southern channel bass are caught on lures and therefore light, one-handed spinning rods and bait-casting rods or popping rods can be used.

When you expect big fish and rough surf, however, and have to cast heavy sinkers, bait, or lures, stick to the heavier outfits. Even on these you'll have your hands full when a big red drum takes hold and tries to cross the outer bar. Many big channel bass are lost each year because the surf angler was using too light an outfit.

When fishing for channel bass with natural bait, use either the standard three-way-swivel surf rig or the fish-finder rig. You tie these with either stainless steel wire leaders or heavy mono leaders. If you expect big bluefish in the surf use the wire. But heavy mono leaders are now favored for channel bass, especially if you expect sharks in the surf and don't want to waste time fighting them on a wire leader.

In northern waters the larger-sized hooks such as the 7/0, 8/0, and 9/0 Eagle Claw, O'Shaughnessy, and Sealey Octopus patterns are favored for channel bass bait fishing. Here you will be using big baits and hooking big fish and need the larger, stronger hooks. But when fishing in Florida, or along the Gulf of Mexico, you can use No. 3/0, 4/0, and 5/0 hooks since the fish run much smaller here and the baits are also smaller.

Mullet, menhaden, or bunker are the baits usually used for channel bass. The mullet is readily available and can be bought fresh or frozen in many fish markets and tackle shops or from bait dealers. Small mullet can be used whole; larger ones can be cut in half, and the big ones can be scaled and filleted or cut into chunks.

Although very good bait for channel bass, menhaden and bunker are difficult to find fresh and even then they tend to be soft baits which spoil quickly and are easily stolen off the hook by smaller fish and crabs. They also tend to attract sharks more than most baits. Thus many surf anglers going after channel bass prefer tougher baits, such as the heads of spot or whiting or croaker. These head sections with some meat attached last longer on the bottom if crabs are eating your bait and you don't have to add fresh bait so often.

Actually channel bass will take almost any fillet, chunk, or strip from almost any fish at one time or another. I've caught small bluefish, cut them into slabs, and hooked channel bass on them. Years ago when the channel bass season opened in the spring North Carolinians used to catch channel bass on hooks baited with salted channel bass put up for eating over the winter months.

Channel bass will also take soft-shell and shedder or peeler crabs. Use a whole crab on the hook and tie it on with thread so it stays on during the cast and while lying on the bottom. Channel bass will also take squid and, at times, clams. In southern waters a whole live or dead shrimp makes an excellent bait. Often combinations of two baits, called "cocktails," work better.

Channel bass will also hit various kinds of artificial lures. One of the best lures is a heavy metal squid or the metal spoon-type lures such as the Kastmaster and Hopkins. The bass will also hit underwater plugs and jigs. Artificial lures are used mostly in northern waters when you actually see the channel bass chasing mullet or menhaden in the surf. But in southern waters such lures are often cast blind along the beaches or from jetties.

You can locate the channel bass in several ways—by watching for birds or gulls diving and feeding on baitfish being chased by the red drum, by seeing baitfish leaping out of the water, or by spotting the big channel bass swirling on top. Sometimes when the surf is clear or when you're looking down from a sand dune or pier, you can see schools of channel bass or two or three of the fish swimming in the surf just beyond the breakers. A few surf anglers who fly light private planes use these to spot the channel bass from the air; then they land on the harder beaches or at low tide to fish for them.

But most of the time channel bass don't reveal themselves, and you have to know or recognize the best spots to locate them. You can look for the sloughs, deep holes, sand bars, and cuts or breaks in the bar and fish these spots. The best sloughs usually have openings on both ends and are fairly deep, with the outer sand bar within casting distance. Fishing in and around inlets and river mouths is often productive. If you are fishing a beach for the first time it's a good idea to get down there at dead low tide. Then you'll be able to spot the bars, sloughs, cuts, breaks, and other bottom formations more easily.

Speaking of tides, you can catch channel bass at different stages, depending on the beach. In some spots fishing is best during the last half of the outgoing and the first half of the incoming tide. At others the last half of the incoming and the first half of the outgoing will produce best. During dead low tide you can often wade through a shallow slough, get up on the outer sand bar, and then cast out into deeper water on the ocean side.

I feel that the time of day is even more important than the tide, especially for the bigger channel bass. You'll find your best fishing will take place around daybreak and for the next two or three hours. After this, it pays to rest up and come back about two or three hours before dusk and fish until sundown. You can also catch channel bass at night, especially around the full moon.

Of course, on cloudy or stormy days you can often fish at any time and make good catches even at midday. When a storm is approaching and the surf is moderate and even somewhat rough, channel bass often move in to the beach to feed. They'll feed even when the water is slightly discolored, and many anglers fishing along the Gulf of Mexico actually prefer a roily surf over a calm, clear one. But along the Atlantic Coast a northeast storm or blow that creates a very rough surf or turns the water brown will usually kill the fishing for a few days until the wind shifts and the water starts to clear. That's a good time to go fishing—right after a storm. The channel bass move in to feed on the uprooted shellfish, crabs, sand bugs, and disabled smaller fish.

A good way to fish a slough with a bait rig is to cast right up the edge of the outer sand bar and let the bait lie there a few minutes. Then lift it sharply off the bottom, reel in a few feet, and let the bait lie for a few more minutes. Keep doing this until the rig and bait are right near the beach. The idea is to cover the entire width of the slough or hole. Sometimes the channel bass will be near or even on top of the sand bar. Other times they will be close to the beach.

If there is a strong current running parallel to the beach you can try holding bottom in one spot. If you can't hold or if you want to cover more territory you can use a lighter sinker and "walk out" a slough. Cast the rig at the upper end of the slough and then slowly keep pace with the bait rig as the current sweeps it down along the bottom toward the lower end.

Some anglers along the Gulf of Mexico in Texas like to use two or three outfits at the same time while fishing for the smaller reds found there. The fisherman holds one rod and the other two rods are placed in sand spikes, in rod holders, or behind the car bumpers of a beach buggy or camper. Of course, you have to set the drag and click loose so that the fish can take some line and you can hear it going out.

When fishing with bait for channel bass you'll do better if you wait until you feel the fish move off with the bait before trying to set the hook. Many times the channel bass will fool around with the bait, picking it up and dropping it, then picking it up again and so on until he finally decides to take it for good. Other times he may pick up the bait, mouth it immediately, and move off quickly. Then you can strike without waiting.

When using artificial lures for channel bass work them deeper and slower than for such fish as bluefish or even striped bass. Metal lures such as squids or Hopkins lures can be cast out and allowed to sink almost to the bottom. Then you can start reeling them back with some rod action, letting them rise and sink so that they flash and shine and look like a slow-moving crippled baitfish.

Once you hook a good-sized channel bass on bait or lures you'll know why he's so highly prized by surf anglers that he's often been called a "bulldog." Channel bass aren't spectacular fighters or even very tricky fighters. They don't leap out of the water or even run as fast as many other species. But they are very powerful, stubborn, persistent battlers that fight right up to the beach. Many big channel bass are lost in the surf when they are horsed or the drag is set too tight. You have to let a channel bass run as often as it wants to. A big fish will make several long runs and many short ones—and in between he may sulk. If you are using light tackle wait him out and don't apply pressure too early or too hard. It may take an hour or longer to whip a big drum on light tackle.

In some states you are allowed to keep only two big channel bass. Even two may be too many, since the big ones are gamey, stringy, and tough and do not make very good eating. The smaller ones, up to about 12 or 15 pounds, make quite good eating and can be filleted and fried in cracker crumbs or cornmeal.

Fishing seasons are important when seeking channel bass and in northern waters they run best in the surf twice a year. The first run starts in March in South Carolina and Georgia and in April along the Outer Banks of North Carolina. In Virginia channel bass show up in May and fishing often continues through June. During July and August the surf fishing slows down; it picks up again in September and October in Virginia and a bit later in North Carolina. In the Tarheel State the fishing is often good in late October, November, and often into December.

But no matter where you fish for them and catch them, you'll soon learn to respect the fighting qualities of the channel bass or redfish, especially when he's hooked in a turbulent surf where he can put up his best fight. After you beach him and admire him why not return him to the ocean to give some other surf angler the same thrill?

BLUEFISH

When surf anglers hear the cry, "The blues are in!" they rush down to the shore because they know from experience that no fish caught in the surf gives you faster or more thrilling action than bluefish. When a school of bluefish tears into baitfish or small fish in the white water, chopping them to pieces, the fishing can be out of this world. Almost every cast brings a hit and, if the blue gets off, more often than not another one will grab the lure.

At such times you'll have no trouble locating the bluefish. You'll see a picket fence of surf anglers lined up almost touching each other, casting, reeling, fighting fish, losing fish, beaching fish, and cursing when lines pop, lures are lost, or fish get off the hook. The commotion and confusion are often comic, but the hard-working surf casters are deadly serious and each man is in a hurry to get his share of fish.

And they often have to work fast, because bluefish usually move in to the beach for short periods, chasing and slashing at the bait, and then move out as quickly as they appeared, leaving you to wait for them to reappear or for a new school to show up. That's because the bluefish is not a true surf fish as is the striped bass or even the channel bass. Most of the time bluefish stay in the deeper water offshore in the ocean, inlets, bays, or sounds, for bluefish are predators, feeding mostly on baitfish and smaller fish. Blues rarely move into the surf unless this food is there to attract them. They are also fast swimmers, very unpredictable in their movements. The runs vary from season to season and from spot to spot. In some places blues appear almost every year in numbers and provide good fishing in season. In other places they rarely show or show only sporadically and runs are undependable.

Bluefish are found in many parts of the world and surf anglers catch them off the coast of Africa and as far away as Australia. Along the Atlantic Coast the extremes of their range are Nova Scotia to Brazil, and they are also found in the Gulf of Mexico. A few bluefish are caught in Maine, but they rarely appear north of Cape Cod in any numbers.

Recent studies have shown that there are two groups of bluefish along the Atlantic Coast. The southern group spawns south of Cape Hatteras; the northern group spawns north of the Carolinas. Their migrations overlap but both groups winter in Florida for their first two years, after which they migrate north.

Around April surf fishing for bluefish begins in the Carolinas and moves north to New York, New Jersey, Rhode Island, and Massachusetts during the summer months. Fishing is often good in these states into the fall, with bluefish being taken from beaches and rocky shores into October. In recent years there have been runs of "jumbo" blues up to 20 pounds or so along the Outer Banks of North Carolina in November and December. At this time the smaller blues also show up in force along Florida's East Coast and surf fishing can be good there all winter long.

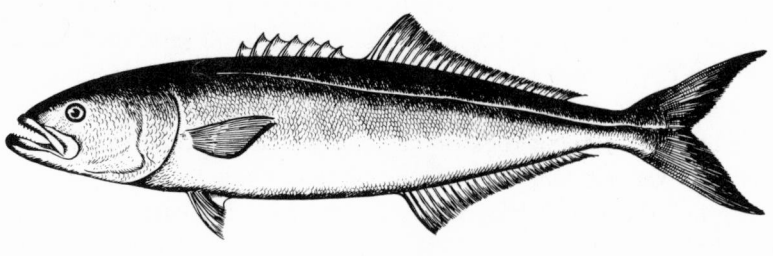

BLUEFISH

As mentioned earlier, when bluefish appear along the beaches in big schools you'll see lines of surf anglers fishing for them. Because bluefish are such sloppy feeders, tearing into the smaller fish and cutting them to pieces, they attract sea gulls and other birds in large numbers. This is one way you can locate the blues. When you see birds working offshore wait until they move in closer to the beach. Often you can see the bluefish leaping out of the water or the baitfish scattering.

Bluefish are particularly active around the mouths of inlets or passes entering the ocean where baitfish get caught in the fast tide and are swept out to sea. Blues also like the deeper dropoffs—holes, channels, and rips, especially rips and turbulent water where currents meet. But they will feed on sand, rock or mussel bars, and other shallow spots if baitfish are taking refuge there. Some good fishing can also be had from jetties, breakwaters, and piers.

You'll often catch bluefish in the rough, white water that striped bass like. In fact, the two fish often feed together, so on one cast you may catch a bluefish and on the next a striper. Some of the best fishing often takes place during northeast storms when such baitfish as mullet, herring, and menhaden get tossed around in turbulent surf. But if the water turns too dirty or too brown it may affect the fishing because the blues may not come to feed.

You can use the same surf fishing tackle for the bigger blues that you use for striped bass or channel bass. Either heavy or medium spinning or conventional surf outfits will serve. But since most of the bluefish taken in the surf will run from about a pound up to 9 or 10 pounds you can use even lighter surf outfits or even one-handed spinning rods or bait-casting tackle when the surf is calm. If you run into blues from 10 to 20 pounds, however, use your heavier surf tackle. I've seen bluefish of 10 to 12 pounds break 20-pound-test line or even straighten out husky hooks when caught in a strong tide or current or heavy surf.

The top lure for bluefish in the surf is a metal squid or heavy spoon-type lure. The Hopkins and the Kastmaster are both excellent. These metal lures come in various weights and you can find a size which the blues will hit. A large single hook is better than a treble hook and many anglers prefer the Siwash or Salmon hook for its superior holding qualities.

Metal lures should be reeled fast to bring strikes from blues on most days. There are times, though, when a slower-moving lure will work best, usually when the blues are not showing on top but are down near the bottom and you have to let the metal lure sink a few feet before you start the retrieve. Most of the time, however, they like a fast-moving metal lure.

Another good lure to use when blues are chasing baitfish on top is a surface plug such as a popper or swimmer. This is also reeled at a good speed to create a splash or commotion. There's no greater thrill in the surf than to have a big blue follow such a plug and make several passes at it before taking it for good. When the blues are not on top, you can often take them on underwater plugs that travel from a few inches to a few feet below the surface.

Bluefish will hit jigs with bucktail, feather, or nylon skirts. Yellow, white, or light blue ones are good, and so are jigs with shiny chrome or silver heads. Bluefish will also go for rigged eels, plastic eels, and eel-skin lures, but the blues' sharp teeth soon chop off or mangle the rigged and plastic eels. If you do use rigged eels, rig them with wire or chain instead of nylon or cord. Eel-skin lures stand up better than a whole eel or plastic eel, but these too should be rigged with wire or chain. Ordinary fishing line or mono line or leader material is easily bitten through by the sharp teeth of the blues. This should also serve as a warning that it's not wise to put your fingers into the mouth of a live bluefish.

If bluefish aren't hitting lures or if you prefer natural baits, you can take blues in the surf on a whole small fish such as a mullet, menhaden, herring shiner, spearing, or sand eel. If the mullet, menhaden, or bunker is big you can cut it into chunks or strips and use these for bait. Mackerel, butterfish, spot, or whiting can also be cut up and used for bait. Bluefish have also been caught on strips of squid, shedder crab, and shrimp at times. For big blues try a live eel either cast out and allowed to swim around free or on a bottom rig with a sinker. It's a good idea to use a two-hook rig with one hook in the eel's head and another one near the tail.

When bait fishing for blues you can use the regular surf bottom rig with a three-way swivel, pyramid sinker, and a 2-foot wire leader to which the hook is attached. Hook sizes No. 4/0 and 5/0 are best for the small bluefish, while a 7/0 or 8/0 hook can be used for the big ones.

Is there a best time of day to fish for bluefish in the surf? Well, like striped bass, blues tend to be most active and come into the white water or close to shore around daybreak, in the late afternoon and evening, and even at night. But there are also times when the blues will feed during the middle of the day if conditions are to their liking. In fact, on cloudy or stormy days when there are plenty of bluefish and baitfish they have been known to feed during a whole tide or even most of the day. At such times you'll actually get tired of hauling in the blues and catches of 30, 40, 50, or even more fish a man are made.

Bluefish hooked in the surf must be fought with plenty of authority but also with plenty of vigilance. They make fast runs, leap out of the water, and try to gain slack line in various ways. One of their favorite tricks is to swim toward you at a fast speed so you have to reel fast or even back up the beach to prevent slack. Keep them coming at all times and feel their weight on the end of the line constantly. But if you do happen to lose the blue, don't moan about it—cast right out again in a hurry and hook another one.

When you catch a bluefish, keep it on ice or in a cool spot out of the sun. It's also a good idea to gut the fish soon after you catch it. Blues' flesh is soft and somewhat oily and spoils quickly, but they make prime eating when broiled or baked.

Some fish caught in the surf put up a feeble or disappointing fight. Not the bluefish! It will fight hard all the way in and even on the beach it will keep bouncing up and down on the sand or rocks. The only time a bluefish gives up is when it dies. And it provides the most sport and fun when caught in the surf.

WEAKFISH AND SEA TROUT

During the 1930's when I first started surf fishing from Long Island beaches, weakfish were numerous and I often took them from the jetties, breakwaters, and beaches. In those days it was often easier to catch weakfish than striped bass, which were relatively scarce compared to the plentiful weakfish. Surf fishers would go out on the big breakwaters at Rockaway Point or Atlantic Beach in June or July and again in September and October, and usually we caught some "tide runners," as the big weakfish were called. Smaller weakfish, of course, were caught in larger numbers than the big ones. And during the fall months many big weakfish were caught by surf casters in front of the lighthouse at Montauk Point and other spots on Long Island and in Rhode Island and New Jersey.

Soon after World War II, however, the weakfish started to thin out along their northern range and soon vanished almost completely from the northern beaches. A few weakfish continued to be caught from the surf along their southern range and as far north as southern New Jersey around Cape May. Now weakfish have made a comeback and have reappeared in numbers in many of their former haunts.

Many old-timers who have caught these fish in the surf welcome their return, because the weakfish is a great gamefish. It hits hard, takes many lures and baits, and puts up a fine scrap on light tackle. And today with spinning tackle it is easier to cast the smaller and lighter lures and baits and have a lot more fun and sport. You also catch many more weakfish on the new lures such as jigs and with the almost invisible lines, which we didn't have in the old days.

The weakfish I've been discussing is the common weakfish or northern weakfish (*Cynoscion regalis*) also known as the gray weakfish, gray trout, squeteague, and salt-water trout. Found from Cape Cod to Florida, it is rather scarce south of the Carolinas. It arrives in northern waters during May, mostly in the bays, inlets, and tidal rivers. A bit later it shows up along the surf and can be caught from jetties and beaches. The smaller weakfish can often be caught throughout the summer, but the bigger fish are usually taken in June, early July, September, and October.

You don't need special tackle to catch weakfish and can use almost any surf fishing outfit you have. But because these fish rarely go over 10 or 12 pounds, use your lightest surf spinning outfits. When fishing in a calm surf from a beach, rocky shore, or jetty you can often use a one-handed spinning rod or bait-casting outfit, both of which are good for casting and working the small lures usually used.

Weakfish will hit many metal lures, such as metal squids and spoons. Years ago a popular lure was a light, flat, metal squid with a long, narrow strip of pork rind attached to the big hook. A

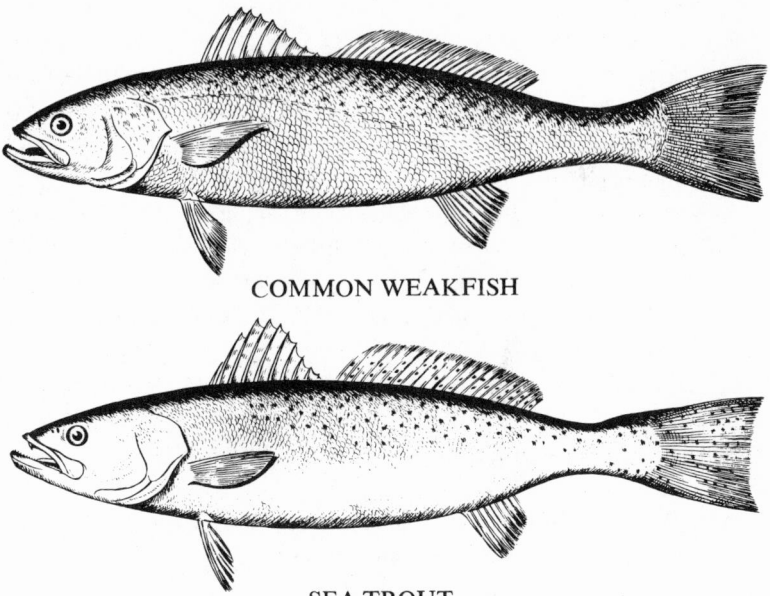

COMMON WEAKFISH

SEA TROUT

small treble hook was slipped on the end of the pork rind. This hooked fish that struck short and helped to hold the weakfish more securely. The only thing "weak" about these fish is their paper-thin mouth; a big single hook tends to tear it and drop out.

Many kinds of metal squids, spoons, and spinners can be cast and used to catch weakfish. Metal lures should be cast out and reeled slowly with occasional speedups or rod action. In deeper water, reached by casting from jetties or breakwaters, you can cast the metal lure out and let it sink while keeping a tight line. Often the weakfish will hit the lure as it is sinking.

Small underwater plugs are also very good for weakfish. Red-and-white or yellow or silver models, either single- or double-jointed, are most effective. These too should be reeled slowly for best results.

The surf angler seeking weakfish has a wide variety of the so-called jigs with bucktail, feather, or nylon skirts or soft plastic tails to choose from. They are especially effective when fished from jetties, breakwaters, or rocky shores where deep water can be reached with a short cast. They also work extremely well in fast tides and currents at inlets and river mouths since they sink quickly and deep. And you can work them along the bottom better than most lures.

When weakfish cannot be caught on artificial lures they will usually take some kind of natural bait in the surf. One of the best all-around baits for weakfish is a strip of squid. For big weakfish you can use the whole head and tentacles of a squid or even a whole small squid. For smaller weakfish a strip about 3 or 4 inches long and about an inch or so wide can be used. Weakfish also bite well on shrimp, shedder crab, and sandworms. Or you can try a strip or chunk of mullet or pieces of spot, croaker, menhaden, or mackerel.

You can use the same standard surf rig or fish-finder rig as for other surf fish. The hooks can be size No. 3/0 or 4/0 for small fish and up to 7/0 for the bigger weaks.

When looking for weakfish in the surf, remember that they prefer somewhat deeper and quieter water than the striper or even bluefish or channel bass. While they will feed in a breaking surf, they tend to avoid water that is shallow or rough. So look for the deep holes, channels, and sloughs when fishing from the beach. Some of the best fishing is had from the jetties and breakwaters; the weakfish can be found cruising up and down along the sides of the rocks. Usually, though, the front of the jetty or breakwater where a rip forms and the water is deeper is the best spot for the bigger weakfish.

The prime time to fish for weakfish is when the tide changes, either at high or low water. They bite during the daytime or at night, but the peak fishing periods are usually around daybreak, in the evening, and during the night. Some fine fishing can be had during moonlit nights when big weakfish seem to be most active and will hit small underwater plugs worked slowly or will pick up a natural bait.

A weakfish puts up a good fight, especially at the beginning when a big fish will make some good runs. The drag on your reel should be set light so the fish can take line freely. Horsing or strong-arming a weakfish is a bad practice; a hook tears out of their soft jaws easily. When fishing from a jetty or high rocks always use a net or gaff on fish over 2 or 3 pounds.

Most weakfish caught in the surf will be on the small side, weighing from 1 to 6 pounds. Occasionally you'll get tide-runners going from 6 to 12 pounds, but such fish have been scarce in recent years. Smaller weakfish make pretty good eating, but they should be kept on ice or frozen because they have a soft flesh which spoils quickly.

The southern weakfish (*Cynoscion nebulosus*) is also known as the spotted weakfish, speckled trout, and sea trout. The last name is prevalent throughout the South and that is what we will call this fish here. Although sea trout may stray as far north as New Jersey they don't really become common until you go to Maryland and from there on south they become more abundant, reaching their greatest numbers in Florida and the Gulf of Mexico.

Like its northern relative, the sea trout is caught more often in sounds, bays, tidal rivers, inlets, and passes and on the inland flats than along the surf. But in many areas good catches are made from beaches, jetties, breakwaters, and piers.

Sea trout are caught all year round in Florida and the Gulf of Mexico. Even farther north in North Carolina, South Carolina, and Georgia you often have good fishing in December; if the winter is mild, they can also be caught in January and February. They run best in northern waters, however, from May to November.

Sea trout travel in good-sized schools and usually there is fast fishing when they appear along the beaches. Like most surf fish they don't stay long in an area or feed too long, but come and go with the tides and the baitfish or other food. When there's a good run of sea trout you'll see anglers lined up along the beaches casting for them.

If there are no anglers fishing you have to locate the sea trout yourself. Look for them in deep holes and sloughs with the outer sand bar not too far away. The best sloughs or troughs will have openings at both ends and will average about 6 feet in depth. If the slough is deep enough sea trout even lie in it at low water and some good fishing can be had.

Although sea trout don't mind some surf, they don't particularly care for very rough or very dirty water. The best fishing takes place when the surf is light or moderate and the water is clear. They hit best early in the morning, toward evening, and at night.

You can use the heavier surf spinning and conventional surf rods when bait fishing with bottom rigs or when casting from a jetty or pier, but you'll find lighter tackle more suitable for these fish. Light, one-handed spinning rods and bait-casting rods or popping rods work best with the light lines and lures. Many anglers even prefer fresh-water rods and lines as light as 4 or 6 pounds on their small spinning reels. Such light tackle casts the smaller ¼ - and ⅜ -ounce lures better and the light line makes it easier to work the lures near the bottom. Of course, such light tackle is most practical when the surf isn't rough or when you're fishing on a jetty or breakwater where there is no surf.

Sea trout will take various kinds of spoons, metal lures, and squids. These cast well and can be worked at different depths to imitate the small baitfish the sea trout feed on.

When the trout are chasing baitfish or feeding on top, you can use the smaller surface plugs—the poppers, swimmers, torpedo or cigar shapes, and crippled-minnow types. Darters are also good. Such plugs work best early in the morning and toward evening when sea trout are more likely to be feeding closer to the surface.

When they are down deeper, use the smaller underwater plugs. One of the most effective is the Mirro-lure, which sinks and has to be worked in a stop-and-go fashion with plenty of rod action. The red-and-white, all silver, or natural minnow finishes are best in these plugs.

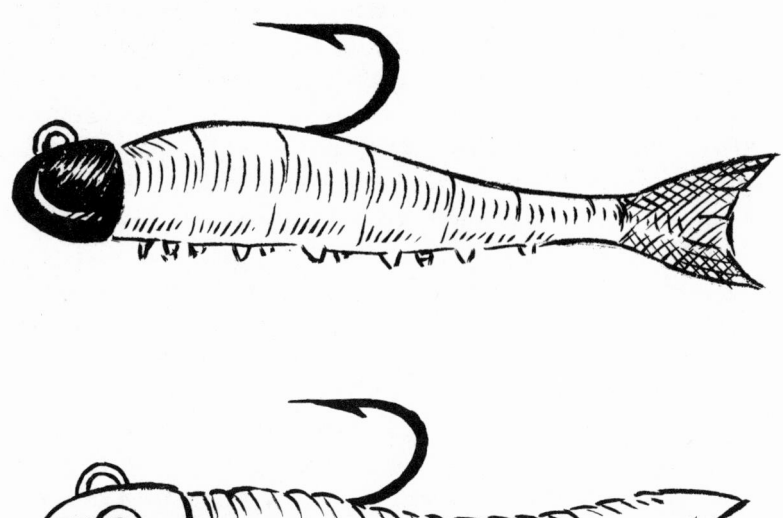

PLASTIC TAIL JIGS USED FOR SEA TROUT

When sea trout are down extremely deep, near the bottom, or when you are fishing for them in strong currents at the mouths of tidal rivers or inlets, you can't beat jigs. Sea trout will take the bucktail, feather, or nylon jigs, but recently those with soft plastic tails have proved most effective. White, yellow, pink, translucent, or natural shrimp jigs are best because they resemble the shrimp that sea trout feed on. The jigs should be worked at various levels, but mostly near the bottom in a stop-and-go fashion resembling the swimming action of a shrimp.

Shrimp is one of the best natural baits for bottom fishing sea trout. A whole live shrimp can't be surpassed for taking good-sized sea trout. You can also use dead shrimp, strips of mullet, menhaden, or other fish. Again, use the lightest surf tackle you can to get the most fun and sport from these light fish. They run from about a pound to 5 or 6 pounds in the surf. They grow to 15 pounds or a bit more but the big specimens are usually caught in the bays, sounds, lagoons, and tidal rivers and even there they aren't common.

Sea trout make good eating, especially the smaller ones. But like most weakfish, they have a soft flesh and should be cleaned early or kept on ice or in a cool spot so that they don't spoil.

15

POMPANO

If the striped bass is the king of the surf and the channel bass is the bulldog, the little pompano is the gold fish of the surf—the most highly prized surf fish caught in southern waters. Except for a few big runs of pompano now and then, the fish is never plentiful. It is also a difficult fish to catch, requiring special bait, a lot of patience, and the luck or skill to be down at the beach at the right time in the right place. Yet the pompano is truly a gold fish because it brings a high price in fish markets and restaurants to the surf angler who sells his catch. For many years the so-called pompano men or pros fishing along Florida's East Coast have been selling their catches to help with their expenses or make a day's pay.

But most surf anglers fish for pompano for sport, fun, and dinner. Many anglers specialize in pompano fishing and even tend to become fanatics about the sport. They remind me a lot of striped bass fishermen up North who fish year after year for stripers but ignore other fish. Pompano enthusiasts act the same way—they'll fish for days, weeks, and even months for pompano and ignore all the other fish running along the beaches.

The reason is easy to figure out. You will often catch various kinds of surf fish even though you may be seeking a specific species, but you'll rarely catch pompano if you're going after something else. If you want to catch pompano with any consistency you have to specialize to a great extent and use the right tackle, rig, hooks, and bait—and fish the right spots.

The right tackle usually means the longest and heaviest surf rod you can make or buy. Pompano fishermen use the longest surf rods on the East Coast, with 12-footers and even 14-footers common along the sand beaches of Florida. Either a long, heavy spinning rod with a big reel filled with 20-pound-test line or a similar conventional rod with revolving-spool reel filled with 30-pound line is needed for the job. You often have to make long casts with 5- or 6-ounce sinkers to reach the pompano; a short, light rod just won't fill the bill.

The pros tend to favor conventional outfits and they often fish with as many as four to six rods stuck in sand spikes along the beach in a hot spot. Pompano usually come in to feed in brief flurries, lasting from a few minutes to a half hour, so naturally the guy with the most lines out will catch the most fish in that short time. Also, the pros don't like to be crowded by amateurs or have their fishing interfered with. By using several rods they give themselves more room to operate in their favorite spot. However, most casual or occasional surf fishermen are better off if they stick to one or two surf rods when fishing for the pomps.

The most popular pompano rig is made by tying anywhere from two to six No. 2, 1, or 1/0 hooks on dropper loops spaced far enough apart so that they don't tangle. A rig with two or three hooks is easier to cast than one which has more. Pyramid sinkers, from 3 to 6 ounces, are used with this rig, depending on the rod used, the thickness of the line, and the surf conditions. The lighter sinkers can be used with the lighter spinning rods and lines on fairly calm days if the fish are feeding fairly close to the beach.

POMPANO

The heavier sinkers are needed for a rough surf and long casts.

The best bait for pompano is the sand bug, called the sand flea by most anglers; this is described in Chapter 5. It's a good idea to get your baits a day or two before you go fishing so that you have them when you need them and you don't have to waste time while fishing. One big sand bug or two or three small ones can be used on a single hook.

If you can't get sand bugs, try pieces of live or fresh shrimp for bait. Two or three tiny coquina clams often work even better than sand bugs in some areas.

Of course, you have to fish for pompano where they are most plentiful, and along the Atlantic Coast this usually means Florida. The beaches along the Gulf of Mexico are also good at times. Pompano do migrate along the Atlantic Coast as far north as the Carolinas and some are caught there in the fall, but they are never plentiful and tend to run small. Your best bet is along the East Coast of Florida from the Georgia border to Fort Lauderdale or Miami; however, the beaches in these big cities are crowded with bathers or surf fishing is not permitted, so you have to go north of Palm Beach to find fishing space.

The pompano season on the East Coast of Florida begins in December and runs into the spring. Along Florida's West Coast and the Gulf of Mexico, the fishing is best in the spring and early summer. But a few stray pompano are likely to be picked up at any time of year in southern waters.

Even during the peak of the pompano season, the fish do not come to feed or bite every day, and they do not feed along the entire beach. Certain spots attract them—the deeper sloughs, holes, and sand bars where the waves wash out the sand bugs, tiny crabs, shrimp, and clams that they feed on. In fact, one way to locate a good pompano spot is to look for piles of coquina clam shells on the beach or fish along the edges of sand bars. Along sharply sloping beaches with no sand bars pompano often come to feed in the breakers right near the beach, but this isn't very common and most of the time it takes a good cast to reach the better sloughs, holes, and sand bars.

Pompano also like to hang around inlets and the mouths of inlets and rivers entering the ocean. You can often find good fishing in the inlet itself, but outside, where the waves break on the sand bars or beach, is usually best. In fact, pompano fishing is almost always better when there is some surf breaking, and anglers along the East Coast of Florida prefer a light or moderate southeast wind which creates some white water. But too strong a wind or storm is usually bad because it turns the water brown or dirty. Then you may have to wait two or three days for the water to clear before the pompano fishing resumes.

When the water is clear it is sometimes possible to see pompano swimming on the bottom. Along the Gulf of Mexico beaches fishermen often locate them this way. A pompano is light, however, and blends with the sandy bottom so it's not easy to spot. By looking for the darker shadow under the fish you can see them more readily, especially if you are wearing Polaroid sunglasses.

Surf anglers fishing for pompano with bait use a special technique that enables the fish to locate the baits quickly. These fishermen cast their baited rig at an angle and reel it in slowly along the bottom, then walk a short distance down the beach and cast in the opposite direction so that the rig crosses the first cast. Then they reel in slowly, again dragging the sinker along the bottom. This forms an "X" on the bottom. Finally the anglers cast once more so that the rig and bait hit and lie at the middle, or cross-point, of the "X." These anglers reason that any pompano swimming along the bottom will come up to the scent of the bait in the sand and will follow it up to the baited rig. Whether it works in practice no one can be sure, but pompano surf anglers have been doing it for years.

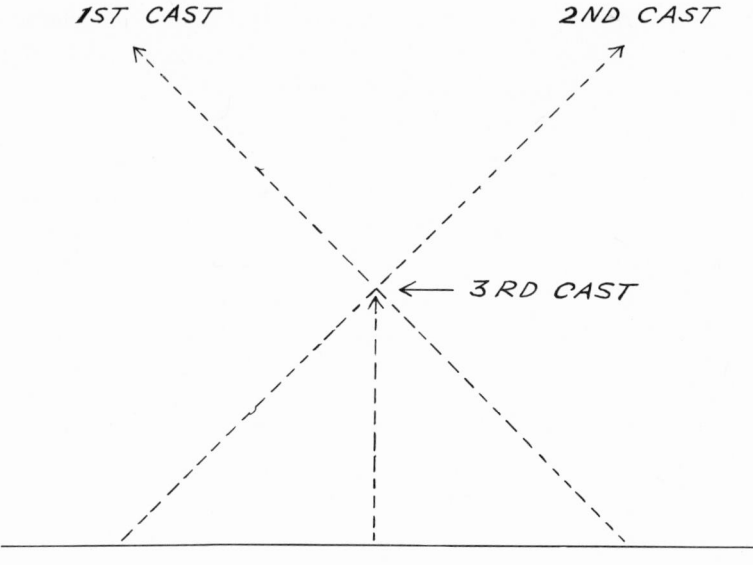

BEACH

THE "CROSSED BAIT TRAILS" METHOD USED WHEN FISHING FOR POMPANO

Pompano will also hit tiny lures such as yellow jigs and have sometimes been caught on tiny spoons or plugs. The jigs are most effective, especially when worked along the bottom very slowly. The trouble with the small jigs is that they are tough to cast any distance from the beach, so they work best when you're fishing from a boat, pier, jetty, or bridge.

You can catch pompano at various stages of the tide although many anglers prefer the last three hours of the incoming tide and the first three hours of the outgoing. High tides are best in shallow spots such as sand bars, holes, or sloughs. But you can catch pompano at low tide in deeper sloughs, holes, dropoffs, and channels.

Pompano can be caught throughout the day, but usually the peaks are at daybreak and toward dusk. Many surf anglers and pier fishermen come down just before daybreak, fish for a few hours, then quit and return an hour or two before dark.

Although pompano do not grow big—most of those caught will run between 1 and 4 pounds—they are tough fighters for their size. If you catch a 10- or 12-pound pompano you have a record fish, but even a small one will bend your rod and refuse to be pulled in without a tussle. They use their broad sides to good effect and remind you of the tough jack crevalle, which is caught in the same waters. But unlike the jack, which isn't popular for food, the pompano is a gourmet's delight when properly prepared.

16

OTHER ATLANTIC AND GULF SURF FISHES

One fascinating thing about surf fishing is that when you cast a lure or bait into the ocean you can never be quite sure what you'll catch. Of course, most of the time you'll be going after a certain species and that is the one you'll usually catch. But you never know when a different kind of fish will suddenly start running. The expert surf angler is familiar with most of the fish that can be caught in his area and he learns which baits, lures, or rigs to use. In this section we will discuss many fish that have been caught from the sand beaches, rocky shores, jetties, and breakwaters along the Atlantic and Gulf coasts.

KINGFISH

The correct name for the kingfish is northern whiting (*Menticirrhus saxatilis*) but along its northern range, especially in New York and New Jersey, it is called "kingfish." Found from Massachusetts to Florida it is most plentiful from New York to Virginia.

Kingfish first appear in numbers along the beaches during May and remain until September or October. The best fishing months are usually from June to September.

In the surf kingfish come in close to the beach in search of small worms, snails, shrimp, sand bugs, and other tiny marine life. They prefer the deeper sloughs, holes, edges of sand bars and channels. They are especially plentiful at the mouths of inlets and rivers entering the ocean. And some of the best fishing can be had from jetties and breakwaters. Kingfish can be caught during the day or night and many surf anglers like to fish for them after dark during the summer months when bathers have gone for the day.

You can use any of your regular surf tackle for kings, but since they are lightweights, rarely reaching more than 2 or 3 pounds, your lightest rods will provide the most sport. Kingfish have a small mouth so a No. 1/0 hook baited with bloodworms, sandworms, pieces of shrimp, shedder crab, clams, squid, or sand bugs should be used.

Kingfish give a sharp, rapid bite—a sort of series of pecks—and you can strike back almost immediately to set the hook. Once they are hooked there is no mistaking them on your line. For a small fish they pull hard, but because they are light they don't fight too long or strain your tackle too much.

A relative of the northern kingfish is the southern kingfish, usually called the "whiting" along its southern range from Virginia to Texas. It resembles the northern whiting or kingfish very closely. It can be caught on many of the baits mentioned above.

All members of this family make fine eating and for food many surf anglers would rather catch them than most other species.

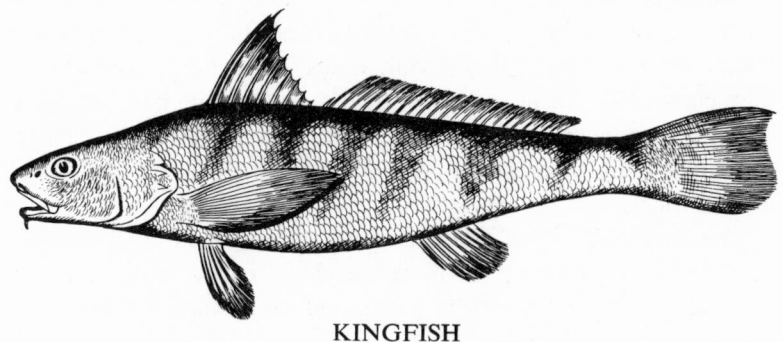

KINGFISH

BLACKFISH

The blackfish or tautog is not a true surf fish, but it has saved many a day for anglers fishing in New England, New York, and New Jersey. Blackfish come close to shore along rocky coastlines and feed near the rocks, jetties, breakwaters, or nearby mussel or oyster beds, where they are within casting distance of the surf angler.

Blackfish are found from Canada to South Carolina but are most abundant from Cape Cod to New Jersey. They come close to shore in late April and early May and there is usually good fishing for them during May and June. In the summer, smaller blackfish are caught near shore, but the larger ones leave for deeper water. They return in September, however, and from then until early November some of the best fishing takes place.

You can use your regular surf tackle for blackfish but the heavier rods, preferably conventional ones, are best. In open water over mussel, oyster, or clam beds with no rocks or just a few small round boulders you can use lighter tackle. But blackfishing is usually best around rocks, and here you'll break off often and lose too much tackle and too many fish if you use light lines. With light tackle you can't keep a blackfish from heading for a crevice and fouling your line.

The best hook for blackfish is the Virginia pattern with No. 6 good for average fish and No. 4 for larger fish. The best baits are fiddler crabs, green crabs, hermit crabs, sand bugs, sandworms, and clams. Blackfish are very clever at stealing bait so bring along plenty, with rigs to replace those lost in the rocks. You'll need plenty of sinkers, too, with the round or bank types best around rocks.

The rocky shores of Massachusetts, Rhode Island, and Connecticut are good spots for blackfish. They can also be taken at Montauk Point and from the jetties and breakwaters along Long Island in New York and in New Jersey.

Blackfish feed in small schools or groups and quite a few will gather in a good spot. The angler who locates one of these spots can often take several fish, while another angler a short distance away will have little or no luck. It pays to try several holes or spots until a productive one is found.

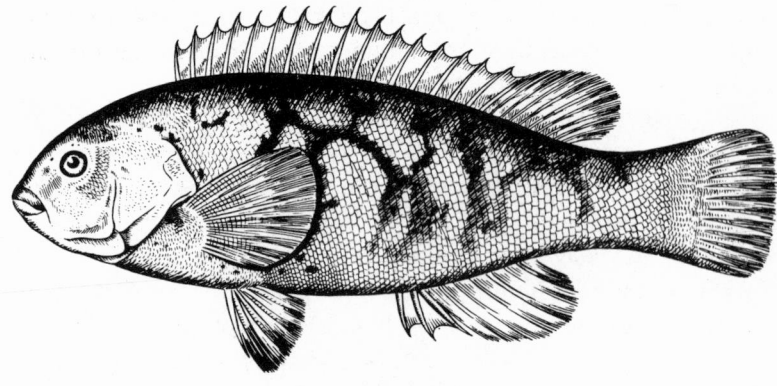

BLACKFISH

POLLOCK

Pollock, too, is not a true surf fish, but when it comes close to shore, it can provide some fast sport. Unfortunately, although pollock are found in deeper waters over a wide area, they are caught from shore or beaches in only a few spots. Maine and Canada are exceptions—from spring to fall pollock are taken in many spots. But farther south they appear mostly at Race Point on Cape Cod, or at Point Judith in Rhode Island, and at Montauk Point, New York. Even at these three spots pollock visits are short and seasonal, with May, October, and November the best months.

Pollock are active, streamlined members of the codfish family. They often feed on smaller fish, chasing them to the surface usually at daybreak or toward evening. This is the time surf anglers catch them by casting small metal squids, spoons, jigs, and plugs. One of the best lures is a splasher wood block with a tiny spoon or jig trailing behind it on a 2-foot leader.

Although pollock don't fight as hard or as long as striped bass or channel bass, they put up a good scrap for a fish in the cod family. They also run to good size and in some places you can get them up to 20 or even 30 pounds.

POLLOCK

BLACK DRUM

The black drum, a relative of the red drum or channel bass, is a deeper-bodied fish and not as red or coppery as the channel bass. When alive they are not really black; they turn this color when they die. Young black drum have vertical stripes that fade with age.

Black drum, especially the big ones, are caught more often from boats, but at times they run along the beaches or can be caught from jetties, breakwaters, and piers. The best fishing is found from southern New Jersey to Florida and in the Gulf of Mexico.

You can use the same surf tackle for black drum that you use for channel bass. Most of the black drum you'll catch from shore will be small, so really heavy surf rods are not required unless there is a run of big drum. Black drum may reach 100 pounds or more and 50 and 100 pounds is common weight, so if you expect these giants use your heavier tackle.

A standard surf bottom rig or fish-finder rig can be used for black drum. The hook can be size No. 3/0 to 5/0 for the smaller fish and up to 8/0 or 9/0 for the bigger ones. Black drum will take clams, shedder crab, shrimp, mussels, and at times cut fish. You can also make a "cocktail" by combining two of these baits on the same hook.

A black drum is slower and not as stubborn a fighter as its relative the channel bass. The big ones are rather coarse and not too good for food, but the smaller ones make fair eating.

The season for black drum starts in northern waters in May and lasts until fall. In Florida and the Gulf of Mexico, they can often be caught the year round.

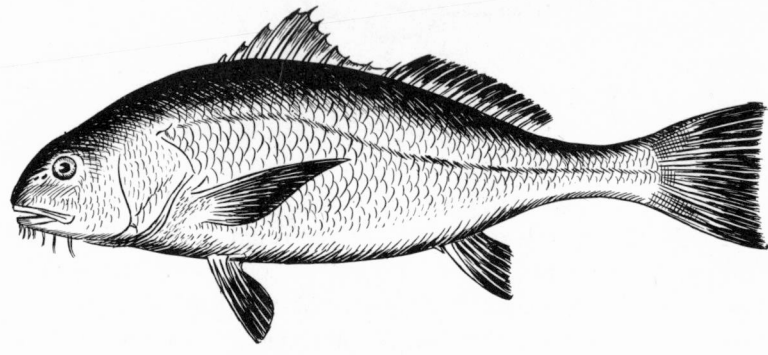

BLACK DRUM

ATLANTIC CROAKER

ATLANTIC CROAKER

The Atlantic croaker, also known as the hardhead, is more often caught from boats or piers, but in some areas and during certain seasons they may appear along the beaches and can be caught in the surf or from jetties and breakwaters. Although they are members of the drum family, they are small, rarely reaching more than 5 or 6 pounds with the average closer to a pound or so. They are excellent eating and are sought as a panfish by many anglers.

Surf anglers will have the best luck for croakers by casting into deep water and holes or inlets and channels. Such spots can be reached more readily from jetties and breakwaters.

Along their northern range in the lower part of New Jersey croakers appear in the summer and fishing in the surf may be good until September. Farther south they may run well in the fall and even during the winter, especially in Florida and the Gulf of Mexico.

Use the lightest surf tackle that is practical and bait the No. 1/0 or 2/0 hook with seaworms, clams, shrimp, or shedder crab. Cast from the beach as far as you can or into deep spots from jetties. If croakers are around you won't have to wait too long for a bite. They run in schools and where you catch one there are usually more. Night fishing is often better than daytime angling.

ATLANTIC MACKEREL

Here's another fish that's more common in the deeper offshore waters, but along its northern range in New England and Canada it often comes in close to shore and can be caught in large numbers from the cold waters along the rocky shores, jetties, and beaches. They run well from June to September with the summer months the best.

You don't need heavy or even medium-weight surf rods for mackerel. Use a light one-handed spinning rod with a small reel filled with 6- or 8-pound-test line for these fish. They'll hit tiny metal lures such as metal squids, spoons, spinners, and jigs.

Mackerel may appear along shore anytime during the day, but the best fishing is usually early in the morning or in late afternoon and evening.

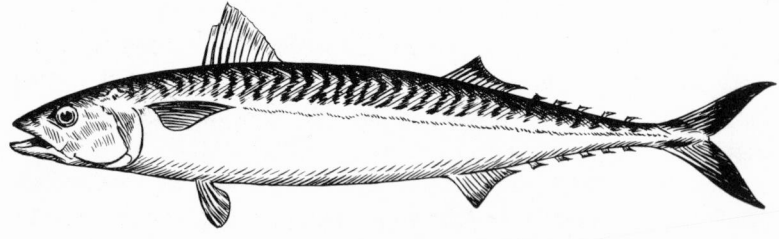

MACKEREL

FLUKE AND FLOUNDER

Fluke and flounder, members of the flatfish family, are sometimes taken in the surf. The flounder most often caught by surf anglers along the Atlantic Coast is the fluke or summer flounder. The fluke is a large, active flounder found from Cape Cod to the Carolinas, mostly in bays, inlets, and deeper waters a short distance from shore in the ocean. But it does come close to the beach or jetties and breakwaters during the summer and early fall and can then be caught by surf anglers. Related species of the summer

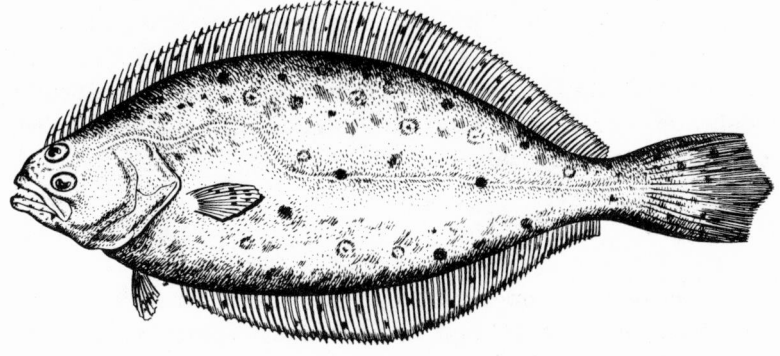

FLUKE

flounder are found farther south along the Atlantic Coast and in the Gulf of Mexico.

Fluke will take a wide variety of baits—seaworms, squid, clams, and small fish. The most common bait is a live killie used in combination with a strip of squid. You can also use small baitfish such as spearing or silversides, sand eels, herring, and shiners. Strips cut from bigger fish or even a strip cut from the first small fluke you catch can be effective.

When fishing for fluke, use a 4/0 or 5/0 long-shank hook on a 3-foot leader tied just above the sinker. The hook is baited, then cast as far as possible. With a live baitfish such as a killie you can let the rig stay in place. But with dead baits you should reel in the rig along the bottom with an occasional slow lift of the rod to give the bait some life and movement.

Because fluke will hit a moving bait more readily than a still one, they sometimes go for artificial lures such as spoons, metal squids, jigs, and deep-running underwater plugs. These lures should be close to the bottom and be retrieved at a slow pace.

The average fluke will run from about a pound to 3 or 4 pounds, but "doormats" weighing up to 10 or 12 pounds are occasionally caught. A fluke can reach more than 20 pounds but specimens above 15 pounds are rare.

The other flounder often caught from shore in northern waters is the winter flounder. They don't run in the surf where the water is rough, but can be caught from jetties, breakwaters, and seawalls in inlets and quiet coves. For them a short piece of bloodworm, sandworm, or a piece of clam or mussel makes a good bait. They run best in the spring and fall months.

SNOOK

The snook is a southern fish that spends most of its time in inlets, tidal rivers, bays, and other inland waters, but in some places and at certain times of the year it does run along the beaches. Then surf anglers go after it and sometimes have good sport. I say "sometimes" because the snook, like the northern striper, is an unpredictable, wary, fickle fish not always easy to fool with an artificial lure.

Snook are found in Florida and along the Gulf of Mexico and other southern waters. When found in the surf, they are likely to be migrating or feeding on schools of baitfish. They are most plentiful near inlets or passes emptying into the ocean and around jetties, breakwaters, sand bars, pier and bridge pilings, where they cruise around or lie waiting for baitfish or shrimp to swim by. They feed on all kinds of baitfish and small fish as well as shrimp. Live mullet, pilchards, and pinfish make good baits.

Surf fishing along Florida's East Coast is best during the summer and fall months, especially during September, October, and November, when mullet are migrating along the beaches. Like the northern striper, they prefer fairly rough water or stormy, cloudy, or rainy weather for their feeding periods. They do a lot of feeding at daybreak, dusk, and during the night.

Snook which run from 2 to 10 pounds can be handled on light or medium-weight surf tackle. But when you expect big ones or when fishing around rocks, mangroves, or pier or bridge pilings, a heavier conventional rod is more practical. Snook grow to 50 pounds or more and many weighing 20 to 35 pounds are caught each year.

Snook will take a wide variety of artificial lures. Surface plugs such as poppers or swimmers are good at times. So are underwater plugs, darters, metal squids, spoons, jigs, and eel-skin or plastic-eel lures. As mentioned earlier, some live baits are very good, but at times snook will also take dead baits fished on the bottom.

A hooked snook puts up a wild and determined battle; even the small ones will often leap out of the water or thrash around on the surface. The bigger ones will give you long runs and try to foul or cut your line on a rock, pier or bridge support, or tangle you in mangroves or other obstructions.

Snook, which have white firm meat and fine flavor, are good eating. The small ones can be filleted, and large ones can be cut into steaks. The snook has been made a gamefish in Florida waters so check size and bag limits before you fish for them.

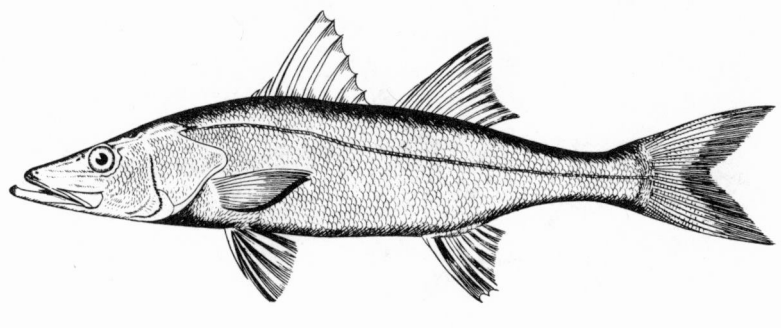

SNOOK

TARPON

The tarpon is another fish which doesn't particularly care for the surf or breakers and prefers the quieter waters of rivers, canals, and bays. However, they may appear off the beaches in some places at certain times of the year. The mouths of inlets, passes, or rivers entering the ocean are the best spots for them.

Although a few tarpon stray as far north as Virginia and the Carolinas and are occasionally caught there from piers, jetties, or beaches your best fishing for them will be in more southerly waters, especially along both coasts of Florida and elsewhere in the Gulf of Mexico. Here they often run from April to November with the summer months the most productive.

The surf angler will have his best fishing from jetties or break-waters early in the morning, toward evening, and during the night. The period around the full moon is a good time. For real sport you can use spinning outfits, but if the tarpon are running big you'll lose most of them. If there's a strong tide or current tarpon will run off a lot of line and you'll often break off. A conventional surf rod is better and will land more fish, especially if you use natural baits. These are usually swallowed and the tarpon is hooked more securely down deep. With artificial lures many fish fail to get hooked or are hooked lightly and get rid of the lure on the first leap or two.

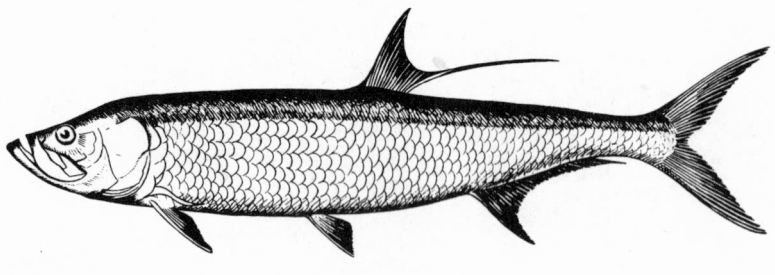

TARPON

Tarpon are noted for their high leaps. They shake their heads violently, land with a loud splash, then leap again and again and fight hard right up to the end. Many lures and rigs will be lost when tarpon break off. Tarpon average from 20 to 80 pounds in the surf, with fish over 100 pounds fairly common.

Tarpon will take such artificial lures as surface plugs, under-water plugs, spoons, metal squids, jigs, and plastic baits. They'll also take natural baits such as live or dead mullet, pinfish, and catfish as well as shrimp and crabs.

The trick is to make a tarpon hit the lure or take the natural bait. Although they are often seen swimming or rolling on the surface, they are not always in a feeding mood. You need plenty of patience and persistence to keep on casting lures, changing lures, and trying at different times until the fish decide to feed.

SHARKS AND RAYS

Sharks are not too popular with surf anglers. When they do appear they steal bait or swallow it and then run out most of your line or break off if they are big. They may bite a hooked gamefish in half after the angler has been playing it or appear in large numbers and chase away the more desirable surf fish.

But a small group of surf anglers enjoys shark fishing and goes after them deliberately. If you plan to do this your best bet is your heaviest surf tackle. A conventional surf rod with a big reel holding a lot of line testing 45 to 60 pounds will give you a better chance of landing the bigger sharks. A few anglers even use big-game rods and 6/0 to 12/0 reels with 80- or 100-pound line. For shark you have to let the bait out in an inlet or river mouth in the current from a jetty. If you fish from the beach, use a big balloon to float the bait out to sea.

Whichever outfit you use you need a wire leader at least 8 to 10 feet long if you want to land these brutes. These long leaders are difficult to cast; one way to handle them is to coil the leader and tie it with a weak cord or tape to shorten it so you can cast it out.

The best fishing in northern waters takes place during the summer and early fall. In southern waters sharks can often be caught the year round. Look for them around inlets, in deep sloughs, along sharp dropoffs, and around jetties and breakwaters.

Sharks will take almost any kind of fish bait, but the oily ones such as menhaden, bunker, mackerel, bonito, and tuna are best.

Use the largest piece you can cast with your outfit or can drift to deep water with a float.

Most of the sharks caught along the Atlantic Coast in the surf will be the brown, black tip or spinner, hammerhead, ground, and nurse sharks. A few other species are hooked at times. With the exception of the mako shark, sharks are not spectacular battlers, but they do have the weight and endurance to make the fight long if the fish is of any size. The secret in fighting sharks is not to let them rest but to make them keep moving so that they tire and you can bring them in.

Sharks will give you the most trouble right in the surf or breakers because here they get the help of the waves and the backwash, putting a strain on your line and rod. Big sting rays will give you even more trouble because their broad, flat surface hugs the sand and makes them difficult to move.

Sharks will be easier to land in the surf if you have the help of another angler with a long gaff. But care should be taken when gaffing or beaching a big shark. An incoming wave may toss the fish toward you and his teeth may take a chunk out of your leg. Never put your fingers into a shark's mouth to remove a hook, even if the shark looks dead.

Sting rays can be caught on the same heavy surf outfits and tackle and on many of the baits used for sharks. They are not too exciting to catch and most surf anglers don't want anything to do with them. They are also dangerous, for a sting ray's tail barb can give you a nasty, poisonous wound.

OTHER FISH

Several other species come in close to shore at times or into the surf and can be caught along the Atlantic and Gulf coasts. The stubborn jack crevalle often chases mullet or pilchards into the breakers and is hooked by surf anglers in southern waters. Also in southern waters an occasional cobia is hooked from a beach or jetty. Cobia run best along Florida's Gulf Coast in the spring.

Spanish mackerel come in close to shore at times in big schools and can be caught on light spinning tackle. The false albacore and bonito have also been caught at times along the Atlantic Coast and in Florida. Other fish include the gafftopsail catfish, porgies, sheepshead, snappers, grunt, and spot.

OTHER PACIFIC SURF FISHES

The Pacific coastline from Washington to Mexico has many species along its beaches and rocky shores. The striped bass is an important surf fish in California, especially near San Francisco, but they run in the surf only for brief periods and other fish have to fill in the slack periods if the surf angler wants to practice his sport most of the year. Luckily, the Pacific Coast angler can find some kind of fish running at any time of the year if he seeks them. We will cover most of these fish here.

SPOTFIN CROAKER

One of the most popular fish caught in the Pacific surf is the spotfin croaker, found from Point Conception to Baja California. It can be caught throughout the year but is most plentiful during the late summer and fall. The spotfin is recognized by its long, pointed pectoral fin with a black spot at the base, where it meets the body.

The best fishing for spotfin croaker is in depressions or deep spots, the so-called croaker holes that are often beyond the breakers and require long casts. These fish frequently bite better at night on an incoming tide. If there is a run of grunion at the same time your chances of catching spotfins are even better.

Many spotfin croaker anglers prefer the two-hook rig, but others make good catches with a single-hook rig on a 3-foot leader. Whichever you use make sure that the hooks are small. Sizes No. 1 and 1/0 are best, baited with mussels, soft-shell sand crabs, clams, shrimp, or seaworms.

The spotfin croaker hits hard and puts up a lively fight for its size. Care should be taken to play the fish lightly, since its mouth is rather soft and easily torn and any slack line will cause the hook to fall out. Most spotfin run from 1 to 3 pounds, with occasional big ones around 5 pounds and a few up to 9 pounds.

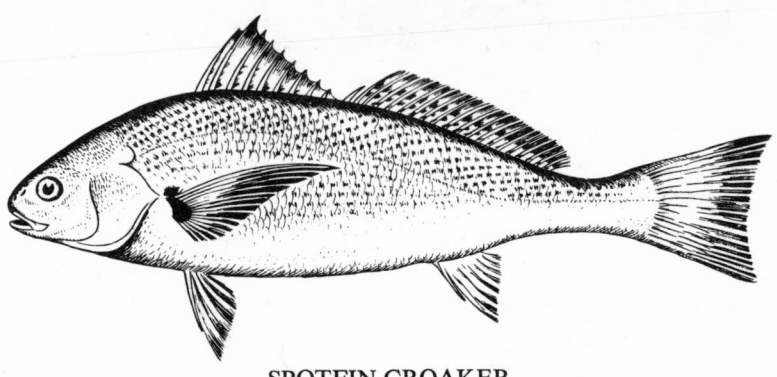

SPOTFIN CROAKER

YELLOWFIN CROAKER

Yellowfin croakers are found along the same general range as the spotfin and in many of the same spots. They can also be caught from jetties and breakwaters, and high tides are usually best.

You can catch the yellowfin on many of the baits used for the spotfin with a No. 1 or 2 hook and the same surf rigs. But yellowfin croakers will also take anchovy and pieces of other fish. Yellowfins run smaller than the spotfin, with a top weight of 3 or 4 pounds.

YELLOWFIN CROAKER

CORBINA

The corbina was once plentiful in the Pacific surf from Point Conception to Baja California. They are still fairly plentiful in Mexico, but catches have fallen off in recent years in California, which means that the surf angler has to work harder, put in more time, and really know his stuff.

The corbina is related to the kingfish or northern whiting found along the Atlantic Coast and resembles it in general shape and outline. In the Pacific it is larger, however, often growing to 2 feet and weighing 8 to 10 pounds. Most of those caught in the surf, though, will weigh from 2 to 6 pounds.

Along their range corbina can often be caught the year round, but the best season runs from July to September. They can be caught on the regular surf tackle used for other surf fish and on similar bottom rigs, but some anglers prefer to use leaders up to 4 feet for corbina. The hook can be size No. 1, 2, or 4. Top bait is a soft-shell crab or bug, but they'll also take ghost shrimp, clams, mussels, and seaworms.

Corbina will often feed close to the beach where the waves break, so avoid overcasting, or at least keep reeling in your rig every so often, letting it lie in one spot for a few minutes before reeling in, with pauses, right up the shoreline.

The incoming tide is good fishing at many beaches, and a couple of hours before and after high tide is also a good time. Night fishing is often better than daytime angling for corbina, as are daybreak and dusk.

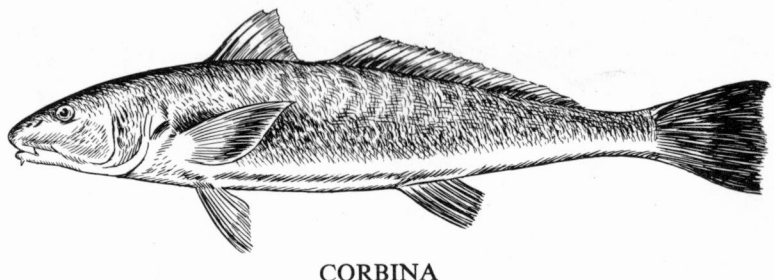

CORBINA

SURF PERCH

The surf perch are a big family with many species found along the Pacific Coast from California to Alaska. They have such names as redtail, barred, striped, silver, white, calico, rainbow, rubberlip, pile, and walleye perch. Some of these are caught along sandy beaches, others are more common along rocky shores.

Surf perch run at various times of the year, depending on the species and the location. In Oregon and Washington the summer months are best, while farther south the winter months can be productive. The best runs in the surf occur when the perch come close to shore to spawn or to feed on clams, sand bugs, worms, or smelt. Try fishing where someone has recently clammed or where smelt are in the breakers. Fishing can be started at low tide; the perch will move in with the tide to feed on the broken clams and other marine life that has been uncovered.

You can also look for sloughs, holes, and depressions in which to cast your baited hook. Fishing from jetties and breakwaters can be very good. Surf perch, depending on the species, will take such baits as razor clams, seaworms, prawns or shrimp, sand bugs, cut smelt, sardine, and anchovy. Most of these fish run small, from a pound to a few pounds, so use No. 6 to No. 1 hooks.

You can also have a lot of fun catching those perch which hit artificial lures. With a light spinning outfit you can try tiny spoons, spinners, jigs, or weighted flies. These are best used from higher elevations such as jetties, breakwaters, or rocky shores.

SURF PERCH

ROCKFISH

Rockfish are another large family, with about 60 species found along the Pacific Coast from the Gulf of California to Alaska in shallow inshore waters and surf to depths of several hundred fathoms, depending on the type. Some of those taken from the surf or shore are the blue rockfish, bass rockfish, black rockfish, kelp rockfish, grass rockfish, bolina, priestfish, scorpionfish, or sculpin.

Most rockfish are fairly small, with only a few reaching several pounds. Since they are usually found around rocks and kelp, however, you usually should use rather heavy surf tackle. Hooks should range from size No. 1 to 5/0 or 6/0, depending on the size and species of the rockfish running at the time.

Rockfish will take a wide variety of baits—clams, mussels, squid, herring, sardine, anchovy, mackerel, and pieces of other fish. These can be fished without a sinker by using a fairly heavy float or bobber about 2 feet above the hook. Cast this out into rocky areas or kelp beds but make sure to clear these obstructions. If you do use weights and fish deeper on the bottom, you can save money by using small cloth bags filled with pebbles as sinkers.

When fishing for rockfish look for rocky cliffs with deep water nearby, kelp beds or patches of floating kelp, tidal pools, or deep holes. You can also fish for rockfish from jetties and breakwaters.

Some rockfish will hit artificial lures such as small plugs, spoons, spinners, jigs, and flies when cast into the deeper spots.

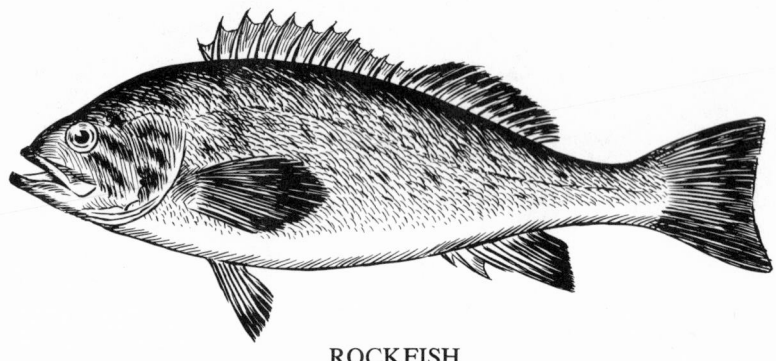

ROCKFISH

SALMON

Although the Pacific salmon is usually taken from boats and the steelhead is caught both from shore and boats in the rivers, salmon can sometimes be caught by surf anglers. The best time to try is when they gather at the mouths of rivers just before they spawn.

The peak fishing usually takes place just before heavy rains open up the river mouths or heavy flood waters come pouring out, permitting the salmon and steelhead to enter the river. You can also have some good salmon fishing during the summer in many places. In the deeper rivers and inlets you can often catch them by casting from jetties and breakwaters in July, August, and September. The fishing can last until November or December.

The fastest salmon fishing takes place when you actually see the fish breaking water and feeding on smaller fish—herring, pilchard, or anchovy—close to shore in the surf or mouths of rivers. Use surf or lighter spinning tackle to cast plugs, spoons, spinners, or similar lures toward the feeding fish. Usually you'll catch the Coho or silver salmon, which comes into shallow water to feed, more often than the larger chinook or king salmon. But you may hook some of these bigger salmon from the longer jetties or breakwaters or in the deeper channels of river mouths. While casting for salmon you may also hook a steelhead, which is the sea-going rainbow trout.

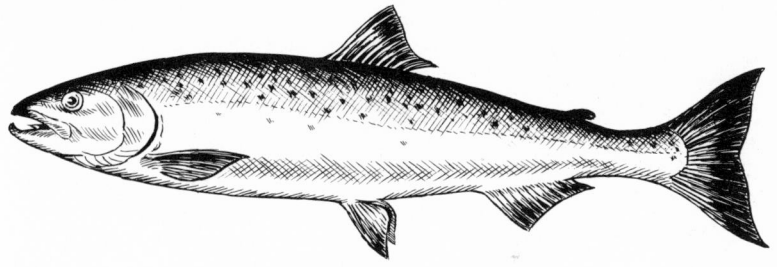

SILVER OR COHO SALMON

OTHER FISH

Surf anglers fishing along the Pacific Coast in northern California, Oregon, and Washington may also catch halibut, ling cod, greenling, cabezone, kelp bass, flounder, and sole. If you fish farther south, in Mexico, you may catch roosterfish, carbrilla, Sierra mackerel, grouper, yellowtail, and other species.

18

SURF ANGLER'S WORKSHOP

Surf fishing is tough on tackle and other gear. Salt water corrodes or rusts metal on reels, rods, and lures; sand, rocks, mussels, and barnacles cut and fray fishing lines. Today's fine fiber-glass rods require less care and maintenance than the old split-bamboo rods, but to get the most use and longest life from your fishing tackle, proper care is necessary. This requires a little time and effort, and the surf angler should get into the habit of working on his tackle and gear at the end of each fishing trip.

Your surf fishing rod should be examined before the start of the fishing season. The warmth and dryness of apartments and homes often loosen the ferrule or reel seat. This can usually be tightened by merely heating the metal over a gas stove or alcohol lamp flame. First, though, it's a good idea to remove the ferrule or reel seat from the rod and heat the part to be replaced over a flame until it is hot. Then spread the ferrule cement over the spot where the ferrule or reel seat goes. Do this while holding the rod high over the flame so that the cement remains liquid. Now force the reel seat or ferrule back into place. The same thing can be done with the top guide if it is loose. You usually don't have to remove this guide—just heat it a bit and let it cool in place.

If you find a lot of play or space between the ferrule or reel seat and the wood part of grip or butt you may have to fill it with cord or thread. Usually about four to six strands of cord cut into short lengths to lay over the wood grip or butt are enough to ensure a tight fit.

If any of the guides on your rod are loose or if your rod requires a complete overhaul because the windings are old or frayed you can strip the guide off the rod and rewind it. The first step is to remove the old wrappings and varnish. Cut the old thread with a razor blade or sharp knife and peel it off. The old varnish can be removed with fine steel wool or sandpaper but before you do this, mark where the old guides were fastened so you can locate the spot again.

To hold your rod while winding on the thread it's a good idea to make a couple of L-shaped wooden corners and cut a V-notch in each one where the rod will be placed. These wooden rod holders can be clamped on both ends of a table. You have to apply some kind of tension to the thread while you're winding. A simple method is running the thread through the pages of a closed book with the spool on the other side; add as many books as you need to get the right tension.

A straight winding job is very simple. The nylon rod winding thread comes in various diameters and colors and can be bought in almost any tackle store. Number A thread is often used for light rods; Number D thread, which is thicker, easier to use, and quicker to wind, is best for heavy surf rods.

You'll need some rubber bands, Scotch tape, or adhesive tape to hold the guides temporarily in place on the rod while winding. They can be easily held by rubber bands while you're lining them up on the rod. When ready to wind, you can hold the guides more firmly in place by wrapping some of the tape around one of the feet of the guides while you wrap the other one.

The only real trick to rod winding is the beginning and end of the wrapping. To begin the winding, tuck the end of the thread under the first few turns and continue wrapping until it is finally buried. To finish off the winding take a short, separate piece of thread, make a loop, and then when you have a few more turns to make to complete the winding, place this separate length of thread over the end of the winding so that the loop extends beyond the last turn. Now wind several more turns over the loop and run the end of the thread through the eye. Take the two protruding ends of the partly buried loop and pull the end of the thread under the last turn, leaving it buried under the last few turns of the winding (see the illustration).

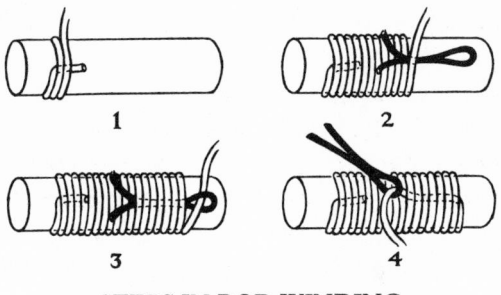

STEPS IN ROD WINDING

The finishing steps call for a comb or rounded piece of plastic or celluloid that can be rubbed over the winding to flatten the thread and fill in the spaces between the strands. Now get some color preservative (sold in most tackle stores) and apply it over the nylon thread. Apply two or three coats, allowing each to dry before applying the next. This will help preserve the true colors of the nylon thread when the rod or winding is varnished.

After the preservative is dry, the rod can be varnished. Use a special rod varnish for this. With a flat, soft brush, apply a light coat, preferably in a warm room free from dust. After the first coat is dry, in a day or so, the rod can be rubbed down with fine steel wool and another coat can be applied. The same procedure is followed between each coat; it usually takes about four or five coats of varnish to produce a smooth protective coating.

You may varnish just the rod windings or thread and not the entire rod, if you prefer; but I think the rod looks better and has a bit more protection if you varnish the entire rod. Modern glass rods do not need as much varnish or protection as did the split-bamboo ones, which often had to be varnished not only at the beginning of the season but also at other times throughout the season, depending on how much fishing you did. With glass rods varnish is really not necessary except to protect and hold the windings in place, and you can go for a few years without adding new varnish.

Many surf anglers make their own rods or actually assemble the rods from parts which can be bought in most tackle stores or ordered by mail. Many companies that sell rod parts also put out complete kits, with instructions, containing all the parts needed to assemble a conventional or spinning surf rod. Thus almost anyone can make a rod and save a few dollars. A one-piece surf rod from 9 to 12 feet long can easily be made from a single glass rod blank just by adding a reel seat, grips, and the guides. Your local tackle store can sell you the parts and also give you some advice on how to assemble a surf rod.

The surf angler who is reasonably handy with tools can also make his own lures. Most surf anglers copy existing models and modify them in size, shape, or color to suit their particular needs or preferences. To make an original metal squid, you first have to carve it from soft wood or mold it from clay. Then you make a plaster cast which is sent to a foundry where a bronze mold is made. This will give you a permanent squid mold from which you can pour thousands of lures.

If you'd like to copy a metal squid you already have, cut off the hook with a hacksaw or file, smooth the rough edges and polish the squid with fine steel wool, and give the lure a light coat of vaseline so that the plaster will not adhere to it. Construct out of thin wood a small wooden box at least ¾ inch wider and longer than the squid on all three sides; on the tail end it should be only ¼ inch longer. In a pinch you can also use a small cardboard box. If you are using a wood frame box get a piece of glass or metal and lay it flat on a table, then anchor the wooden frame to the glass or metal with clay or putty. Now place the metal squid in the center of the frame with the flat side facing down. Make sure the tail end of the squid, where the hook was, is only about ¼ inch from the frame.

Now mix some plaster of Paris in a small pot or can. When you mix the plaster break up all lumps by feeling around with your fingers. This is important, for otherwise the cast will be imperfect. Pour the plaster into the frame until the squid is buried at least ¾ inch and wait for the plaster to harden.

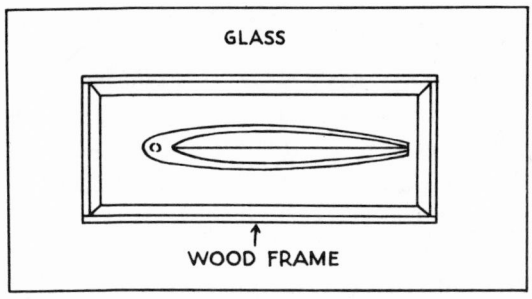

GLASS

WOOD FRAME

METAL SQUID READY TO BE CAST

After about 15 to 20 minutes break open the frame and remove the cast. You may have to slide it off instead of lifting it off. With the point of a knife loosen the squid pattern from the cast and take it out carefully so you don't chip the plaster cast. It will take several days for the plaster to dry. You can speed this process somewhat by baking the cast in an oven for an hour or two.

As soon as the cast is dry, carve a pouring hole in the head end of the cast where the eye will go and cut a small slot for the hook on the other end. When doing this, keep trying the hook you will use in the slot so that it fits tightly and stays in place. You can now use the plaster cast as a temporary mold to make a few squids if you place a flat piece of metal against it. You can use a clamp to hold both sections together while you're pouring.

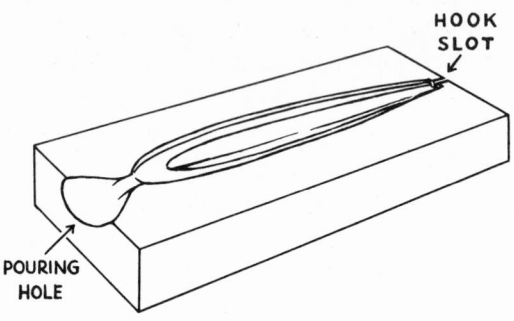

FINISHED PLASTER CAST

Block tin is the best metal to use for pouring squids. It melts quickly, is soft, and has a white silvery shine which lasts even in salt water. Unfortunately, it is difficult to get now and is expensive when you do find it. Junk shops may have some block tin pipe or chunks which you can buy, but the supply is limited. You can also buy bars of solder in a hardware store; this contains some tin but is largely lead. Today most surf anglers use lead for pouring metal squids. This metal is fine, but it turns black in salt water and even when exposed to air, so the squids are usually plated or chromed. You can spray lead squids with silver, aluminum, white, or yellow lacquer or paint them with enamel, using the same colors.

Whatever metal you use, you need a ladle in which to melt it and from which to pour it into the plaster mold. Make sure the plaster cast is completely dry before doing this, or the metal will splatter all over the place. Usually you can make anywhere from six to a dozen metal squids from a plaster mold before it breaks up too much.

If you want to make a permanent mold, do not use the plaster cast. Instead, send it to a foundry and have a bronze copy made. When this metal mold comes back, it will be rough and require some finishing which can be done with a flat file on the outside surfaces and a small three-cornered file on the inside. If you have a small electric grinding tool you can use this instead and do a quicker, better job. Finish the mold by polishing the inside with emery cloth and then crocus cloth to smooth it.

Next, cut a slot in the tail end of the mold for the hook or the eye, depending on whether you want a stationary or swinging hook. The slot should hold the hook firmly in place when you're pouring the squid. Some surf anglers even make a tiny vise on the end of the mold to hold the hook in place.

Use a flat metal plate about the same size as the mold to cover it. If you have the necessary drills, taps, and tools, you can fasten hinges to the cover and mold and add two handles. In the meantime you can use the mold if you get a small clamp to hold the cover in place when you're pouring.

Some mail-order houses sell molds for metal squids, jigs, or sinkers. These molds are relatively inexpensive when you figure that they will last for years and you can pour thousands of sinkers or lures. Some of them, such as the sinker and jig molds, have anywhere from two to five cavities and thus you can save a lot of time.

After you cast the metal squid or jig, you can tie bucktail, feathers, nylon, or plastic around the hook. Usually white, yellow, orange, red, or blue skirts or any combinations are best for surf fishing. After these are wound around the hook, the wrapping should be coated with clear lacquer or varnish.

Many surf anglers also like to make their own wooden or plastic plugs. If you have a small wood-turning lathe you can easily make all the plugs you need. The best wood for plugs is cedar because it is easy to work, resists moisture, and has good buoyancy with the added weight of the hooks and metal parts. It is a bit on the light side for distance casting, however, so many surf anglers prefer ash, cypress, or birch for plugs.

You can fasten hooks to a plug quickly with screweyes, but they should have a long thread and be thick and strong enough to hold a big fish. Brass eyes will last longer in salt water but are not as strong as steel. You can also fasten the hooks to the plugs with metal saddles held in place by two screws. The most secure way to fasten the hooks, however, is to drill a hole the entire length of the plug and run a heavy wire through it. Then drill other holes on the underside of the plug into which you can insert swivels holding the hooks. The wire will run through the eyes of these swivels.

You can buy ready-made wooden or plastic plug bodies and most of the metal parts and hooks needed to make plugs from mail-order houses such as Herter's, Netcraft, or Finnysports.

If you have a spray gun, use it to paint the plug bodies any color you want. Lacquers and enamels in spray cans can also be used to produce a quick finish, or you can brush on a coat of enamel. Usually the best procedure is first to give the raw wood or plastic body of the plug a base coat of white lacquer or enamel and then add the other colors.

When making lures buy the strongest and best hooks you can find. Surf fish run big at times and tiny hooks straighten out, often costing a good fish. For surf or salt-water fishing get tin- or cadmium-plated hooks. Stainless-steel hooks are available, but they cost more.

Keeping your fishing tackle and lures in good shape and ready for instant use is very important in surf fishing. During the off season when there is no surf fishing in your area go over all your tackle and lures to make sure that they are in good condition.

After each fishing trip, your tackle should be washed or cleaned. Fishing rods can be rinsed under a hose or wiped with a wet or damp rag. Metal parts such as the reel seat and guides require more attention than the glass rod.

Surf fishing reels, both conventional and spinning, should also be washed with fresh water or wiped with a damp rag. After that spray the reel with a rust preventive or oil, or soak a rag in oil and wipe the reel lightly.

For a thorough cleaning, take the reel apart and wash it in kerosene, gasoline, benzine, or turpentine. A stiff brush or even an old toothbrush can be used to get into tight spots to remove dirt, grit, and sand. Use a good oil or grease that is recommended for fishing reels to lubricate the moving parts as required. Special care should be given to the bearings in which the spool revolves in conventional reels. These usually require oil before, and often during, a lengthy fishing trip or when you cast a lot. In spinning reels the line roller and the handle knob require oiling often. In fact, handle knobs on all reels should have a light grease or oil applied frequently so they function smoothly and don't wear.

At the end of a fishing season, it's a good idea to send your reel to the factory for a complete checkup and overhaul if necessary, or you can take it to a local dealer who does this work. Then you will be all set for the coming season with a smooth-working reel that won't let you down at a critical moment.

Nylon, Dacron, or other synthetic fishing lines require less care than the linen lines of the past. They don't have to be dried after each fishing trip, but they should be examined before use to see whether they have been nicked, frayed, or weakened in any way. It's also a good idea to keep the reels in solid containers or out of the sun's rays, for light may deteriorate a nylon monofilament line.

Fishing lures should also be examined before the fishing season starts and between fishing trips during it. Badly rusted or weak hooks and metal parts should be replaced. Worn-out hooks should be replaced with strong new ones, some of which have a split or open eye to make this easy. Other lures may have to be taken apart before you can add the new hooks. You can also coat your hooks with oil or even spray them with lacquer to help prevent rusting.

All this care pays off in the long run. When you hook a big fish in the surf, it's comforting to know that your tackle is in top condition. The careless or lazy angler who neglects his tackle often winds up losing a big fish—one that he may have spent years searching for—so give your surf fishing tackle the good care it deserves.

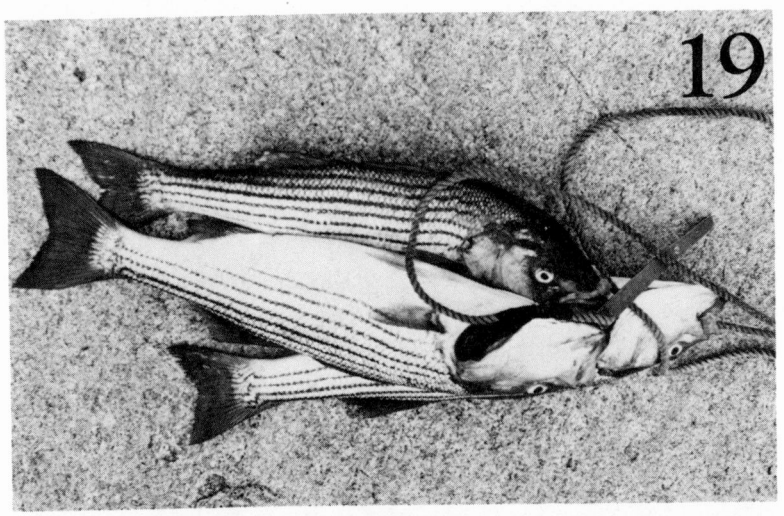

DANGERS, MANNERS, CONSERVATION, AND SPORTSMANSHIP

Surf fishing is a tough, rugged sport at times with dangers and hazards that the wise angler avoids or takes precautions against. The constant danger in surf fishing is the surf itself. Waves can wash you off a jetty or rock or knock you down. The most treacherous waves are the quiet ground swells that loom up suddenly and hit you with the full force of tons of water. One rule to be observed at all times is, "Never turn your back on a wave!"

When you are contemplating fishing a certain low rock, a jetty, or a rocky shore always wait at least 15 or 20 minutes before you go out. Usually there's a lull of a few minutes when the waves are smaller, then you get three or four big ones. If you rush right out on a low rock during the lull you may find yourself hit by the next series of big waves and washed off the rock. So wait to see where and how high these big waves are before venturing out on a low rock.

Then there's the danger of being trapped by an incoming tide on the end of a jetty, sand bar, or reef. Study the local tide tables so you know when low water occurs and the tide changes and you can get off before the tide traps you.

Most jetties and rocky shores are slippery at low tide, when the moss-covered rocks are exposed. It pays to wear ice-creepers or wading sandals with hobnails or spikes. This is especially true at night, when you can't see which rocks are best to walk on. Since surf anglers do a lot of fishing after dark, you should also have a good light for walking on slippery rocks or climbing jetties. The best light is one that hangs around your neck and leaves your hands free for fishing and holding on to a rock or other support. A light also comes in handy when you're landing or gaffing a fish at night or removing hooks or lures from its mouth.

Surf casting today at the more popular, crowded spots can be hazardous because so many anglers are casting all around you. Watch out for the "side-swipers" who swing the rod sideways or use a long lead from the rod tip to the lure. Stay away from them or, even better, avoid fishing crowded spots. And when you're ready to cast, always look behind you to make sure no one is there.

The fish themselves can cause trouble with their spines, fins, or sharp teeth. Striped bass have sharp dorsal fins that can puncture your waders or boots and pierce your leg. Bluefish, sharks, and barracuda can bite your fingers or hand. All active fish can be dangerous when you're removing a hook or lure, for they may jump or twist and drive the hook into your hands. Hit a fish on the head with a billy or club to stun it or pin it down to the ground with your leg before trying to remove the hook.

Surf anglers are always being hit by waves, getting caught in a shower, or finding their boots or waders filled with water, so it's a good idea to carry an extra pair of dry pants, shirt, sweater, and .socks for a quick change. This is especially true in the early spring and late fall or on a cold day or night.

Despite the dangers surf fishing is a relatively "safe" sport compared to many others. If you know the dangers and take steps to avoid them or prepare for them you'll usually have no difficulties.

But there are other problems. Our growing population, expanding cities and suburbs, networks of highways, and new homes, buildings, industries, and other developments have created many of them. The number of surf anglers, for example, has increased in recent years. Not too long ago you could go down to a beach even on a weekend and find plenty of fishing space, especially if you drove some distance from the larger cities. But today you run into many other surf anglers also looking for a spot to fish. On weekends and holidays, most of the popular surf fishing spots are crowded—especially if fish are running—so crowded, in fact, that it takes some of the joy out of fishing.

What aggravates the situation is that while the number of surf anglers is increasing, the beach areas where you can surf fish are decreasing. Now you run into many beaches that are fenced in and surrounded by signs declaring "No Trespassing," "Private Property," "Keep Off," and "No Fishing."

Cities, towns, and private individuals are slowly but surely taking over our wilder beaches. Today, instead of finding sand dunes and miles of uninhabited beaches, the surf angler is more likely to find himself fishing with boardwalks, stores, hotels, apartments, homes, highways, and other signs of civilization and so-called progress in the background. Only a few beaches are still wild and many of these are threatened. Luckily a few national parks and state parks have been created in some areas and these usually permit surf fishing. But we'll need a lot more surf fishing space in the future.

During the summer months the surf angler is also constantly harassed by bathers, surfers, skin-divers, lifeguards, police, and property owners if he tries to fish during the day. He even finds that some of the best spots are closed to surf fishing. The result is that surf anglers are practically forced to fish late at night or around daybreak or before or after the swimming season. Even along the beaches where he can fish unmolested he often finds parking a big problem. If he tries to find a spot to park near the fishing area, he often runs into restricted zones and "No Parking" signs.

Not only are the beaches shrinking or vanishing but the spread of cities, towns, industries, and homes has resulted in the filling in and draining of marshes and bays. These shallow waters are sanctuaries for young gamefish and baitfish, nurseries where they can live, feed, grow, and replenish supply. As more and more inland wetlands are filled in or drained, there will be fewer and fewer fish.

Pollution has taken its toll of gamefish, baitfish, and other marine life and reduced the total fishing space. Many beaches near our larger cities and towns are so badly polluted that fish avoid them. Even if you do catch a fish brave enough or foolish enough to swim into such waters it isn't fit to eat. Such fish as striped bass enter rivers in search of brackish or fresh water to spawn. If the mouths of these rivers or the rivers themselves are badly contaminated, the fish may not be able to spawn in them. Dams, too, prevent fish from going upriver to their spawning grounds.

Commercial fishing continues to deplete the number of surf fishes in many areas. Recently, an increasing number of states have passed laws protecting striped bass from netting, but seining is still permitted in some states and big hauls of female stripers are made each spring, fall, and winter. The snook has been made a gamefish in Florida and the striped bass has been protected in California for many years, but as both the sports fishermen and commercial fishermen continue to catch certain species, the supply is sure to diminish and the result will be poor surf fishing. And now we even have to worry about foreign fishing boats that drag the bottom or net along our coasts. They make big hauls of certain fish which feed in the surf.

There are no easy solutions to these problems. Many coastal states and organizations and the Federal Government have started research projects in an effort to find answers. A lot of information is available and some is being put to use. But before we get real results, much more research is needed, in addition to better enforcement of fishing laws, supervision of commercial fishing, more patrol boats, more game wardens, and limits on the number of fish which can be caught. All such programs taken to conserve our fisheries and fishing should get the full support of every surf angler. Individual surf anglers can help but even more effective are the efforts of surf fishing clubs and various sportsmen's and conservation agencies.

There's no doubt that the increase in anglers and the decrease in fishing areas have resulted in crowded conditions along many beaches. Shorter work weeks, extra holidays, growing wealth, more cars, and a greater awareness and appreciation of the outdoors have encouraged more people to take off and go to beaches to fish or indulge in other water sports.

All this calls for more cooperation and sportsmanship among surf anglers. Unfortunately, many newcomers to the sport are not familiar with the unwritten rules and ethics of surf fishing and often spoil the fishing for other anglers.

Every surf angler should try to live up to the unwritten laws and ethics of the sport. One rule is that the man who arrives first on the scene is entitled to his spot and should not be crowded. Many surf anglers, especially beginners, have no idea how much space is required for safe, comfortable, and productive surf fishing.

Along an open sand beach, the angler who just arrives should stand at least 50 feet away from the nearest fisherman. Those anglers who have done a lot of pier or party-boat fishing may wonder why so much space is required in surf fishing. When casting lures or bait, a surf angler doesn't always want to cast directly in front of him. Every so often he likes to cast to the left or right at an angle and fish different spots. Also, if a strong wind is blowing from the side, his cast or his neighbor's cast may land far to one side, often tangling lines. And if a big fish is hooked, he may start running sharply to the left or right and into the line or rig of the next angler and so lose his fish. Thus, another rule of surf fishing is that if the angler next to you hooks a big fish, you reel in your line to give him room to play the fish. If you are fishing some distance from the lucky angler you can usually reel in quickly enough, but if you are too close, you may not be able to reel in before the fish crosses your line. This is another reason why you should keep your distance and not crowd the angler fishing near you.

Of course, certain hot spots have acquired a reputation and, being human, surf anglers try to get their share of fish and crowd shoulder to shoulder, into a small stretch of beach. On jetties and breakwaters some crowding is usually unavoidable, especially if there is only one rock pile or only a few jetties in the area. But even here, on the shorter, smaller jetties there is room for only one or two surf anglers on the end. The rest of the anglers should fish the sides, a good distance from the anglers up front. Anglers arriving later should stand a similar distance behind those already near the front. If you insist on going up front and standing close to the other anglers you are asking for trouble—casting is difficult and dangerous in such close quarters and you may get caught on somebody's hook.

Some surf anglers will say, "But the other anglers have the best spots—they are catching all the fish and we aren't getting any. I have a right to fish there as much as anyone else!" This may be true, but it is no excuse for bad manners or poor sportsmanship. When the fish are running in the surf, they usually spread out along the beach and your chances are as good, if not better, down the line. You'll have less competition from other surf anglers in less crowded spots and usually catch more fish. Besides, in certain spots there is only enough room for a certain number of anglers. If it isn't too crowded they all catch fish, but if too many anglers try to crowd into the spot they may ruin the fishing for everybody.

Before you crowd another surf angler ask yourself: "Will I interfere in any way with his sport?" "Will I cramp his style and be casting in waters he may want to fish?" "Will I be endangering this angler with my casts?" If the answer to any of these questions is "Yes" good sportsmanship requires that you move to another spot.

Many anglers who haven't done much surf fishing fail to appreciate the benefits and appeal of the sport. One of the basic appeals is that you have plenty of elbow room and water to fish. You must also get a chance to relax. Many surf anglers come down to the beach to get away from traffic, crowded cities, noise, pollution, and people. There are times when a man wants to be alone to think, relax, and forget about business, work, his family, or personal worries. Surf fishing can give you this opportunity, but not when anglers insist on crowding. Then you can't call it surf fishing anymore—in fact, you might as well be on a crowded party boat, pier, or bridge pushing, shouting, tangling lines, and having a hectic time. If you like that kind of fishing and those crowds, then stick to it. But if you want the restful, soothing solitude of surf fishing, broken only by the cries of a seagull or the breaking of a wave, then learn to respect the rights of others to enjoy the same things.

Because of overcrowding and the uncertainty of success, many veteran surf anglers tend to be reticent and may seem unsocial. If they have caught some fish in a certain spot, they keep it a secret. They know that once the word gets out, the spot will be crowded and they will have to fish somewhere else. You really can't blame a man for not revealing where he caught his fish. It's not because he wants to be selfish or greedy and keep the place all to himself— he'll often tell a friend or two where he got his fish and extend an invitation to come along the next day. But he knows that if he tells a stranger or too many people the word will spread and in a short time a hundred anglers may be trying to fish a spot where there is room for only three or four.

However, once you have done some surf fishing, you'll find that most surf anglers are friendly and will gladly help a fellow sportsman. There's no sport like surf fishing for making friends. The pleasures gained in meeting new anglers who become through the years old friends is really gratifying. If you walk along any beach and stop to chat with a surf angler you'll usually get a hearty welcome. Most surf anglers enjoy swapping information and ideas with other surf anglers—quite a few will even give you tips and hints that will help you catch fish.

Surf anglers also respect each other because they know that it's a rough, tough game and anyone who catches fish from the beaches, jetties, or rocky shores works for his catch and knows his stuff. They also know that there are easier and better ways to catch more fish in salt water, but realize that the true surf angler doesn't always expect to catch fish. Even on the days when he draws a blank he gets enjoyment from the booming surf, the white beaches, rocky shores, the breaking waves, the color of the water, the sky, the clouds, sunrise and sunset, and the gulls and other sea birds. All this helps form a common bond among surf anglers and there's a spirit of harmony and camaraderie not often found in other kinds of fishing.

SURF FISHING SPOTS

Here we'll give you a rundown state by state of the best and most popular surf fishing spots along the North Atlantic and Pacific and Gulf coasts. Naturally, runs of surf fish vary from year to year and season to season; the fact that a certain spot was good last year doesn't necessarily mean that it will produce again this year. Most of the spots listed here have been fairly consistent through the years and bear watching or should be fished every so often to see whether any fish are running.

MAINE

Surf fishing has never been fully developed in Maine and the angler has a lot of territory he can explore. Most striper fishing in Maine is done in the rivers, bays, and marshes, but there are many sandy beaches, rocky shores, and islands which can be fished if you can get to them. Mackerel can be caught almost anywhere from shore during the summer months. Pollock, flounder, and tautog or blackfish can also be caught in many spots.

Striped bass and some of the fish mentioned above have been caught at Popham Beach, Walter Reid State Park, Higgins Beach, Old Orchard Beach, Ocean Park, Camp Ellis, Parsons Beach, Kennebunk Beach, and York Beach.

The mouths of most rivers entering the bays or ocean can also be fished for striped bass and other Maine fish. Among these are the Belfast, Darmariscotta, Kennebec, Morse, Scarboro, Saco, Kennebunk, Mousam, Ogunquit, and York rivers. The best months for surf fishing in Maine are June to October.

NEW HAMPSHIRE

The coastline of New Hampshire is short, but there is some surf fishing at the mouths of the Hampton and Piscataqua rivers and you can fish from shore for striped bass in the rivers themselves. You can also fish Rye Beach, Hampton Beach, Seabrook Beach, and the beach at Rye Harbor State Park. The summer and early fall are best for catching striped bass, mackerel, pollock, and an occasional Coho salmon.

MASSACHUSETTS

Massachusetts ranks high among the states where you can catch striped bass from the surf. Cape Cod has miles of beaches which can be fished, and a beach buggy comes in handy here for reaching most of them and covering all the hot spots. These include Race Point near Provincetown, Race Point Lighthouse, Peaked Hill, North Truro, Wellfleet, Orleans, Nauset Light and Inlet, Chatham and Monomoy Island, all famous for surf fishing. In addition to stripers, you'll catch bluefish at some of these spots. And in the spring pollock can be taken at Race Point.

The Cape Cod Canal can also be fished from shore although there isn't much surf there. But striped bass can often be caught by casting from the rocks lining the banks of the canal, especially early in the morning, at dusk, and during the night. Bluefish are also caught here in some years.

There is also some surf fishing from the beach along Plum Island in the extreme northeastern part of Massachusetts.

The offshore islands of Martha's Vineyard, Nantucket, and Cuttyhunk are famous as striped bass spots; some of the biggest stripers are caught here from boats. But many spots in Martha's Vineyard such as Gay Head, Squibnocket, Katama Opening, Wasque Point, and Menemsha can be fished from the beach and rocks. Bluefish are also caught from these islands and the best surf fishing runs from June to October.

RHODE ISLAND

Rhode Island may be a small state but it offers some of the finest surf fishing along the Atlantic Coast. It is famous for its big stripers, but surf anglers can also catch mackerel, pollock, weakfish, tautog or blackfish, and fluke or summer flounder from its rocky shores, beaches, and jetties. In the Newport area you can fish such spots as Sachuest Point, Land's End, Easton's Point, Brenton Point, and the rocks along Ocean Drive. If you cross over to Jamestown, you can fish most of the southern half of the island; Beavertail is especially good.

On the mainland of Rhode Island starting a few miles north of Narragansett Pier we find Anawan Cliffs, Frenchman's, Fort Varnum, the Clumps, Narrow River, Dunes Club Beach, Ocean Drive, Monahan's Cove, Flat Rock, Hazard Avenue, Newton Avenue, the Swimming Pool, Wanamaker's, Nathan's Cove, Black Point, Stewart's Stinky Beach, Sheep-pen and Point Judith. These are mostly rocky shores with cliffs, boulders, points, coves, ledges, and reefs that produce many stripers and other surf fish.

Along the south shore of Rhode Island we find more sandy beaches and here you can fish Matunuck Beach, Green Hill, Charlestown Beach, and Breachway, East Beach, Quonochontaug,

Weekapaug, Misquamicut, Watch Hill and Napatree Beach and Point.

Some years there is also good surf fishing on Block Island. At the extreme northern end of the island Sandy Point is a productive spot for striped bass and bluefish. You can fish most of the southern half of Block Island starting at Dickens Point on the western side and down to Southwest Point, Black Point Rock, Mohegan Bluffs, Southeast Light and Point, and up to the bathing beach at Old Harbor. The summer and fall are best in Block Island.

CONNECTICUT

The shoreline of Connecticut is fairly long, but it borders Long Island Sound so unless there is a strong wind blowing from the sound toward shore there is little or no surf. However, there is some shore fishing from beaches, rocky points, breakwaters, and around river mouths for striped bass, bluefish, mackerel, tautog or blackfish, and flounder. Access may be difficult to many of the better spots, and parking restrictions discourage a lot of shore fishing in this state.

Fish have been caught from shore around Greenwich and Stamford at Greenwich Point and Shippan Point; around Westport at Burial Hill Beach, Compo Beach, Bedford's Point, and Schlates Point; in the Bridgeport area at St. Mary's Seawall, Seaside Park, Fairfield Beach, Breezy Point, and Pleasure Beach; in the New Haven area at Prospect Beach, Savin Rock, West Haven Beach, and Morningside; at Hammonasset State Park at Megg's Point Breakwater, and at Waterford, near New London, at Harkness Memorial State Park.

NEW YORK

New York surf anglers are fortunate in having Long Island's south shore, which is lined with beaches and jetties. Starting near New York City we find the Rockaway Point Breakwater, Jacob Riis Park, Rockaway Beach, Atlantic Beach, Long Beach, Lido Beach, Point Lookout, Short Beach, Jones Beach, Tobay Beach, Gilgo Beach, Cedar Beach, Fire Island State Park, Great South Beach, Moriches Inlet, Westhampton Beach, Hampton Beach, Tiana Beach, Shinnecock Inlet, Southampton Beach, and most of the stretch running east to Montauk.

Montauk Point itself is famed for its striper fishing and bluefishing and here such spots as Shagwong Point, North Bar, Evans Rock, Jones Reef, Scott's Hole, the Lighthouse, Turtle Cove, Caswell's, Frisbies, Coconuts, Ditch Plains, Dead Man's Cove, and the rest of the beach running west to Hither Hills can be tried.

Some spots along the north shore of Long Island facing Long Island Sound can be fished from shore. Here again, there is no ocean surf, but when the wind blows strong from the north, northwest, or northeast you can get some surf in spots. But fish such as striped bass, bluefish, weakfish, blackfish, and flounders can often be caught even when there is no surf. Some of the better spots are Matinecock Point along Bayville, Lloyd Point, Eaton's Neck, Sunken Meadow State Park, Crane's Neck, Rocky Point, Herod Point, Roanoke Point, Horton Point, and on out to Orient Point.

NEW JERSEY

In New Jersey starting from Sandy Hook in the north and running south to Cape May are miles of beaches and jetties which surf anglers can enjoy. Parking and fishing may be restricted during the summer months and bathing season in many places, but plenty of spots can be fished at daybreak, dusk, and night as well as before and after the swimming season. Sandy Hook State Park is a good place to fish, and you can continue down to Seabright, Monmouth Beach, Long Branch, Elberon, Deal, Asbury Park, Belmar, Spring Lake, Manasquan and the Inlet there, Point

Pleasant, Seaside Park, Island Beach State Park, Barnegat Inlet, Long Beach Island, Beach Haven, and most of the inlets and outer beaches from Atlantic City to Cape May.

Depending on the season you'll catch striped bass, bluefish, weakfish, fluke, blackfish, kingfish, and croaker.

DELAWARE

Most of the Delaware coastline fronts Delaware Bay and only a short stretch of beach runs along the ocean to the Maryland state line, where some surf fishing can be done. Here you can fish Cape Henlopen State Park, Rehoboth Beach, and the section of public beach from Rehoboth to Indian River Inlet. The jetties at Indian River Inlet can be fished, as well as the beach south to Fenwick Island. You'll catch striped bass, bluefish, weakfish, fluke, kingfish, and croaker.

MARYLAND

Maryland is another state with a short coastline, and surf fishing is confined to this stretch. Most of the beach from Fenwick Island to Ocean City and from there south along Assateague Island to the Virginia border can be fished for striped bass, channel bass, bluefish, weakfish, kingfish, and croaker. The best fishing is usually during the spring, late summer, and fall.

VIRGINIA

The outer barrier islands, which are the best surf fishing beaches in Virginia, can be reached only by boat from the mainland. However, you can reach the lower half of Assateague Island at Chincoteague by road and fish quite a few miles of beach there, or you can fish in the southern part of the state at Virginia Beach, where a good highway runs along the ocean. The best channel bass fishing is found on such outer islands as Smith, Fisherman's, Myrtle, Ship Shoal, Cedar, Metomkin, Assawoman, Parramore, Hog, Cobb, and Wreck. Other fish caught in the Virginia surf include black drum, striped bass, bluefish, flounder, weakfish and sea trout, croaker, and kingfish. The best fishing is in the spring and fall for channel bass and striped bass, but other species are often caught during the summer.

NORTH CAROLINA

North Carolina is extremely fortunate in that it still has many miles of wild beaches that can be fished by surf anglers for a variety of species. A beach buggy is definitely an asset here to reach some of the better spots. Except for a few isolated islands that must be reached by boat or plane, most of the North Carolina beaches are accessible by good roads, especially the long stretch from Kitty Hawk to Ocracoke. North of Kitty Hawk you can take gravel or dirt roads up to Duck and Corolia and fish the beach here. From Kitty Hawk south to Kill Devil Hills, Nags Head, Whalebone, and Oregon Inlet is a highly developed section with motels, tourist attractions, and restaurants and summer homes. Surf fishing can be done from many of the beaches and piers here for channel bass, bluefish, weakfish, sea trout, and kingfish or whiting.

Once you cross the bridge at Oregon Inlet you are on Hatteras Island—one of the best surf fishing beaches in North Carolina. Here you can fish such spots as Rodanthe, Waves, Salvo, Avon, Cape Hatteras, and around Hatteras and the Inlet. Also some piers along this stretch can be fished. Channel bass, bluefish, sea trout, some striped bass, whiting, bonito, and sharks are usually caught on Hatteras Island.

Crossing Hatteras Inlet by ferry we come to Ocracoke Island. The entire length up to Ocracoke Inlet can be fished, with North Point and South Point the most productive spots.

South of Ocracoke we find the Core Banks, with Cape Lookout, a wild stretch requiring a boat from the mainland to reach the better spots. Here you'll catch channel bass and most of the other North Carolina surf species. Fishing is especially good here for weakfish and sea trout.

Bogue Banks to the west has Atlantic Beach, Salter Path, and Emerald Isle. Running south of here are numerous islands and inlets down to New Topsail Beach, Wrightsville Beach, Wilmington Beach, Cape Fear, and the South Carolina state line which can be reached by road or boat.

North Carolina surf fishing is best in the spring and fall for channel bass and bluefish. Whiting or kingfish bite the year round. Weakfish, sea trout, and the few stripers that are caught bite best in the late fall and early winter.

SOUTH CAROLINA

The surf fishing in South Carolina hasn't been publicized very much but it is often good from the beaches and islands that can be reached by road or boat. Starting in the north we find Waiter Island and Bird Shoal near Little River, North Myrtle Beach, Myrtle Beach, Garden City Beach, Pawley's Island, Cedar Island, Murphy Island, Cape Island, Cape Romain, and Bull's Island. The last two places have excellent fishing for channel bass in the spring and summer and are part of the Cape Romain National Wildlife Refuge. They can be reached by boat from Moore's Landing. Continuing south we find Caper's Island, Isle of Palms, Kiawha Island, Seabrook Island, Edisto Island and Beach, Pritchard Island, and Hilton Head Island.

Besides channel bass you'll also catch bluefish, sea trout, black drum, sheepshead, pompano, whiting, and spot.

GEORGIA

Georgia is another state with some good surf fishing along its beaches but here again most of it is found along the outer islands accessible only by boat. Savannah Beach in the northern part of of the state and St. Simons Island and Jekyll Island can, however, be reached by roads. You can fish about 10 miles of beach at the Jekyll Island State Park. If you can get to Skidway Island, St. Catherine's Island, Sapelo Island, Wolf Island, Little St. Simons Island, and Cumberland Island you can often find good fishing for channel bass, bluefish, sea trout, pompano, jacks, and whiting along the outer beaches or the sounds or inlets between the islands.

FLORIDA

Florida has many miles of fishing beaches on both the East Coast facing the Atlantic Ocean and on the West Coast facing the Gulf of Mexico. Starting in the north on the East Coast you can fish from Fernandina Beach down to New Smyrna Beach with some good fishing from the beaches and jetties for black drum, channel bass, tarpon, cobia, sea trout, sheepshead, and whiting.

Just below Cape Kennedy you can fish many beaches from Melbourne to Fort Pierce if you follow Route A1A and can find parking space. Sebastian Inlet and the inlet at Fort Pierce are good spots for fishing from the jetties and breakwaters. Along this stretch you'll get channel bass, tarpon, sea trout, bluefish, pompano, snook, jacks, and whiting.

Just south of Fort Pierce you'll find Hutchinson Island, one of the best surf fishing areas along Florida's east coast, especially at Jensen Beach and St. Lucie Inlet. Bluefish and pompano are caught here during the late fall, winter, and spring. Tarpon, snook, and bonito run well during the summer. Other times of the year you may catch channel bass, sea trout, whiting, and Spanish mackerel.

South of here we find Jupiter Island and Juno Beach, where you can fish in some sections for the same fish caught just north of there. From here on south we come to the "Gold Coast" area of Florida, highly developed and crowded with tourists and bathers. Thus surf fishing space is limited or restricted. You can fish from some of the jetties at Boynton Beach or Boca Raton or a few of the public beaches early in the morning or late at night, but your best bets are some of the piers along the Gold Coast down to Miami.

Shifting to the west coast we find plenty of beaches, both wild and developed, and some of these can be fished. There isn't too much surf along the Gulf of Mexico in southern Florida and many of the best surf fishing spots have to be reached by boat. Islands and passes or inlets such as Cape Romano, Sanibel Island, Captiva Island, Gasparilla Island, Peninsula Key, and others provide good fishing for channel bass or redfish, tarpon, sea trout, and snook from the beaches.

But the better surf fishing along the Gulf of Mexico is found in Florida's northwest sector at Panama City, St. Andrews State Park, Destin, Fort Walton Beach, and Pensacola Beach on Santa Rosa Island. Along this stretch you may catch channel bass, cobia, sea trout, pompano, whiting, bluefish, and jacks from March to November.

ALABAMA

Alabama has a short coastline fronting the Gulf of Mexico and surf fishing is limited to such spots as Gulf Shores, the beach from Gasque to Fort Morgan, and Dauphin Island reached by Route 163 from Mobile. Along these beaches you may catch channel bass or redfish, sea trout, pompano, sheepshead, croaker, and jacks.

MISSISSIPPI

Mississippi is another state with only a few beaches that can be fished. The best fishing is found on such offshore islands as Cat Island, Ship Island, Horn Island, and Petit Bois Island. Except for Ship Island, which has a ferry running to it during the summer, most of these islands have to be reached by boat or plane. Many of the species found in the Gulf of Mexico can be caught from these islands.

LOUISIANA

Because the Mississippi River enters the Gulf of Mexico through the central part of Louisiana and forms the vast delta region, the fishing here is mostly in the bayous, bays, rivers, or marshes. However, there is some good surf fishing on some of the islands here if you can get out to them by boat or plane. The Chandeleur Islands are particularly noted for their channel bass or redfish, sea trout, pompano, and flounder.

Another good surf fishing spot, Grand Isle, can be reached by a highway and several miles of beach here can be fished for channel bass, pompano, and sea trout. In the western part of Louisiana you can fish the beach from Cameron to Sabine Pass at the Texas border for many Gulf species.

TEXAS

Texas has a long coastline with many beaches and islands which can be fished in the surf. Some of these must be reached by boat while others are connected by bridges and highways. Many of the beaches are undeveloped and a beach buggy is needed to get to the more remote spots.

Starting in the east we find a good stretch of beach from Sabine Pass to Port Bolivar that can be fished in the summer for sea trout, sand trout, croaker, and gafftopsail catfish. During the fall you can catch good sized channel bass, and in the late fall and winter whiting and sea trout run well here.

You can cross from Port Bolivar to Galveston by a free ferry and fish Galveston Island and down to Brazosport and Freeport. Farther down you'll find Matagorda Peninsula and Matagorda Island and St. Joseph Island with many miles of wild beaches that can be fished but they are accessible only by boat.

A causeway from Corpus Christi will get you to Port Aransas and Mustang Island. Beaches and breakwaters can be fished for tarpon, channel bass, sea trout, croakers, Spanish mackerel, flounder, cobia, and even jewfish and sharks off the jetties.

Finally we come to 115-mile-long Padre Island, which can be reached from Corpus Christi at its northern end and from Port Isabel at its southern end. Here you have one of the top surf fishing spots in Texas. Most of the beach is wild and will remain that way because it is in the National Seashore Preserve.

Depending on the season you'll catch channel bass, sea trout, snook, pompano, whiting, croaker, bluefish, black drum, gafftopsail catfish, jacks, sharks, and rays from the beach here. Padre Island is a narrow strip of sand and if the fishing in the surf isn't good you can walk over to the Laguna Madre side and try your luck there by wading or from a boat.

Finally we come to the Mexican border and here the mouth of the Rio Grande can be fished for tarpon, snook, redfish, sea trout, and other species from April to November, the best surf fishing season in Texas.

CALIFORNIA

California has a 1,200-mile shoreline along the Pacific Ocean, most of it paralleled by highways, making many fine surf fishing spots accessible. In the north much of this coastline is rocky with high cliffs, but there are also some sand beaches which can be fished.

Starting at the extreme north around Crescent City and traveling south to Eureka we find such spots as the Redwood National Park, Trinidad Beach, and Humboldt County Beach Park. Here and between these spots you can try for ling cod, cabazone, greenling, rockfish, and surf perch. Striped bass have been sighted along this stretch and some have been caught but fishing for them is better farther south.

The coastline from Cape Mendocino south to Jenner has such spots as Rockport, Fort Bragg, Mendocino, Manchester Beach and Point Arena, Anchor Bay, Sea Ranch, and Fort Ross that are close to Route No. 1 and can be fished for many of the species mentioned above.

From Jenner near the mouth of the Russian River south to San Francisco you can try for striped bass. Big stripers do go up the Russian River and have been caught from shore and boats for several miles up the river. Good surf fishing spots south of Jenner include Sonoma Coast Beach, Ocean View, Dillon Beach, Point Reyes, and Stinson Beach.

Around San Francisco we come to the best surf fishing area for striped bass in California. Here you'll find such spots as Baker's Beach, Thornton State Beach, Pacifica, Sharp Park Beach, Montara Beach, Half Moon Bay Beach, and Pescadero Beach, all of which have had good runs of striped bass during the summer months in the past.

Farther south toward Santa Cruz and Monterey you'll catch some striped bass along the shore of Monterey Bay near the mouth of the Salinas River, but this area is better for rock bass, cabazone, surf perch, kelp bass, and snapper. From Monterey south to Lompoc near Point Conception you'll catch many of the same species along miles of scenic beaches and shore.

From Point Conception to Los Angeles many beaches and jetties can be fished for kelp bass, corbina, yellowfin croaker, spotfin croaker, sculpin, cabazone, bonito, mackerel, halibut, and surf perch.

Many of these species can also be caught south of Los Angeles down to San Diego. Here you can try Hermosa Beach, Redondo Beach, Long Beach, Newport Beach, Laguna Beach, San Clemente Beach, San Onofre Beach, Oceanside around Del Mar and Torrey Pines, and on down to Imperial Beach just north of the Mexican border.

OREGON

Oregon has excellent fishing for striped bass in Coos Bay and River but this is mostly from boats. Some striped bass have been caught in the ocean just north and south of Coos Bay. Humbug Mountain State Park is a good spot to try. Oregon has many beaches, rocky shores, jetties, and state parks that can be fished for such species as cabazone, rockfish, greenling, and surf perch. You can also try for salmon and steelhead at the beaches, rocks, and jetties at the mouths of many rivers entering the ocean.

WASHINGTON

Washington is similar to Oregon in that it has miles of beaches, rocky shores, and jetties or breakwaters that can be fished for the same species. The breakwater at the mouth of the Columbia River can be fished for salmon, rockfish, and perch. The beaches north of here such as Long Beach, Grayland, Ocean City, and Copalis can be fished for surf perch. And in the north you can fish in the Strait of Juan de Fuca from the Oregon shore for salmon, ling cod, flounder, rockfish, and other species.

HAWAII

This chain of volcanic islands is popular with local surf anglers, who fish from some of the sand beaches, rocky cliffs, and rocky ledges that border the deep water surrounding them. The better spots, such as Lare Point on Oahu and Bamboo Ridge near Honolulu, are often crowded with as many as fifty heavy surf rods lined up and stuck into holes dug in the rock. Some of these spots are difficult to reach and require tricky descents and hard climbs. However, there are easier and safer spots to fish from sand beaches and along coral reefs if the surf is not too rough.

The most important surf fish in Hawaii is the ulua, which is a member of the jack crevalle family. They often reach 40 or 50 pounds and occasionally go over 100 pounds. They usually bite best at night when the sea is choppy, and small, whole octopus or the tentacles of larger ones are used as bait.

Another fish often caught from the surf along sand beaches or from rocky points is the bonefish. They run big in Hawaiian waters, with fish up to 10 or 12 pounds often taken, and they reach 20 pounds or more in weight. The best months to catch them are from December to April. Early morning and evening incoming tides are most productive. You cast out as far as possible with a hook baited with a slice of octopus, crab, or shrimp.

Other fish caught from Hawaiian surf or shores include the barracuda, moi, manpachi, goatfish, and threadfish.

CANADA

Canada has some beaches and limited surf fishing, but it does have many miles of shoreline and inlets and bays where you can fish from shore for various species. On Vancouver Island, for example, you can often catch Coho or silver salmon casting from shore. Here the western side of the island is best and you can also try the river mouths and inlets for salmon or steelhead.

Going over to the Atlantic side you'll find some surf fishing for striped bass in New Brunswick, near St. John at Negro Point Beach. The St. John River can be fished from shore for striped bass right in the heart of the city at Reversing Falls and farther inland.

Nova Scotia offers the surf angler or shore angler many beaches, rocky shores, river mouths, and bays that can be fished for striped bass, big pollock, and even cod. The summer and early fall months are best here.

MEXICO

The surf angler lucky enough to get down to Mexico can fish for many miles on remote and undeveloped beaches. On the Gulf of Mexico side below the Texas border and running down to Veracruz you can try for channel bass, snook, sea trout, jacks, and tarpon.

If you can get over to the Yucatan Peninsula and Quintana Roo you'll find fabulous fishing from shore for tarpon, snook, bonefish, permit, barracuda, and jacks. The water is so clear here you can usually spot the fish and then cast to them.

On the Pacific side of Mexico you have so many beaches and shores to fish along the mainland in the Gulf of California or Sea of Cortez and the Pacific Ocean you can spend a lifetime exploring just the better spots. Both sides of Baja California can be fished from various beaches and rocky points or cliffs. Here you're likely to catch yellowtail, sea trout, Corbina, cabrilla, roosterfish, pompano, Sierra mackerel, grouper, and jacks.

INDEX